THE UNENDING LOVE OF A FATHER

The Unending Love of a Father

Copyright © 2017 Moreale P. Brown

Printed in the United States of America
ISBN 978-1-946425-06-5

Book design by CSinclaire Write-Design
Cover design by DGuevara Traffic Peddlers

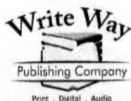

Write Way
Publishing Company
Print . Digital . Audio
Write Way Publishing
Company LLC

THE UNENDING LOVE OF A FATHER

A model of a true and loyal father for a new perspective on living a life of freedom, happiness, forgiveness, love, confidence, and security.

Rev. Moreale P. Brown

Write Way Publishing Company LLC

TESTIMONIALS

It was truly a blessing to read God's word as spoken through a true servant. Men need to know this perspective, which every man has asked himself time and time again as he grows in the Lord.

— Stephen Wright
Charleston, South Carolina

Father God has empowered Rev. Moreale P. Brown to write this book that will help dads to become fathers and fathers to become godly fathers. This is the prophetic hour for godly fathers to take their rightful place in their children's lives (Malachi 4:5-6). Men have been crying out to the Lord for help in how to be godly fathers, and this book is the answer.

— Dr. Jacqueline Williams
Charlotte, North Carolina

As I have read this book, I found a deep relationship in our understanding of the compassion and intimacy of the father, Jehovah God. It demonstrates His deep love for mankind. This book is a step-by-step plan that God instituted through the various covenants and dispensations that have taken us to a point of eternal blessings and rewards. Your life will be enhanced when you read about God's love and plan to reconcile individuals, couples, families, youth, and children back to a healthy relationship with their eternal father, God.

Douglas Nelson
Master's degree in Biblical Studies/Theology
Charlotte, North Carolina

DEDICATION

*This book is dedicated first to my mother for all the
strength and love she showed me and to all of the
fathers of the world who are struggling to be
a part of their children's lives.*

❧❧

*May the Father of mercy comfort you, give you peace,
and lead you to mend difficult relationships.*

ACKNOWLEDGMENTS

I thank my Heavenly Father for the passion He gave me to know Him and to share the treasure of His teachings that all may see God in the context of their family.

Special thanks to my mother, Albertha Brown-Gaillard, my father James Brown, and to my supportive family and friends.

I am extremely thankful for these Shepherds: Pastor Johnny and Stacey Brown, Dr. David and Diane Demola, Apostle Johnnie L. Washington, and Rev. Clifford and Marjorie Johnson.

My gratitude is to my inspirational leaders: Mrs. Sharon R. Neilson, Ms. Lucille Mullings, and Rev. Dr. Jamillah Mantilla.

I am also grateful to the faculty at Faith International Training and the Tabernacle of Prayer Bible Institute.

Finally, I am thankful to my reviewing editors, Mrs. Chakula S. Johnson, MBA, Margaretta Young, and Mr. Donald Young; Clive Malahoo for his technology help; to Write Way Publishing Company; and to those who contributed in typing, advisement, prayers, support for completing this book, and to the volunteers of Christ's Ambassadors Ministries.

CONTENTS

Fatherhood and the Relationship Circle

Strategies that will bring back the "fire" in your marriage
and strengthen your family

A good father made some bad mistakes yet God gave him
grace

Break unwanted cycles in your families

Moses —a foster child who became a great leader

God looks at your heart

A good life on earth and an inheritance for Israel and the
Christians

Rev. Moreale Brown through the guidance of the Holy Spirit has looked into society and taken on the challenge of doing research and written a document that is so needed for this century. I am convinced that Satan is at war with families and is taking an aggressive posture against the roles and need for fathers in the household. The research findings that she states are staggering. The fact that 24 million children in the United States are apart from their biological father is mind boggling. Further, as one seriously considers this breach, you begin to realize the social ills that result from a broken family system. A broken family system creates havoc in society and prevents our communities from developing into an environment that produces positive results.

Rev. Brown is correct as she challenges the reader to become a champion and break the cycles of father-lessness. In my years of experience as a Pastor, I have always felt that God was looking for champions and that people were crying out for one. Much of the negative behavior that we witness results from people crying out for something that they are missing within. In many cases this cry is for the love and attention of a father. Further, this can be seen in our churches as people, male and female, who have not had the experience of a father seek out persons that can fill that void in their lives. I believe that if a man truly loves God, he will give of himself to become a champion in someone's life and exhibit a moral and spiritual posture that represents a Godly father. This in turn will be a blessing to those living without the knowledge of or not in relationship with a biological father. It will also be a visible example to all as to the role that fathers play in the life of a family.

This book explores the need for fathers in a meaningful and informational way. It traces fatherhood all the way back to the Patriarchs and shows the role that fathers played in God's creation and order. Rev. Brown in a unique way shows that persons who are committed to eliminating social ills can do so by following the patterns that were established by the Patriarchs and God's other servants. She further informs the reader that it requires the cooperation of the faith community, systems, and agencies if effective change is going to take place. Rev. Brown's emphasis on the subject should cause the Pastor to look beyond Sunday morning and move toward engaging these partners as part of a movement to restore Godly families.

The good news is that this book says to those with no hope that there is hope. The writing of this book is a gift to persons that are sincerely following God and looking for tools and resources to strengthen families, and all of us should take the journey.

Rev. Dr. Clifford I. Johnson
Pastor, Shiloh Baptist Church
Wilmington Delaware
April 18, 2017

God, are you real?

During my tenure at Bethelite Baptist Church, I recall Rev. Clifford Johnson proclaiming that God is the God of Abraham, Isaac, and Jacob. At the tender age of 12, I began to ask myself how the Bible related to real-life situations. I asked the leaders, but I wasn't satisfied with the answers I received. I still did not see the connection from the Bible to my life.

Leaders, this is the age that "tweens" and teens become curious about life and begin to ask questions about religion. We need to be ready to give them meaningful answers for their own lives. As a result of my questioning experience as a tween, I told my mother that I no longer wanted to be in the choir. *This was the beginning of my backsliding.*

The backsliding first started in my mind, and then my actions followed my thoughts. The church leaders were shrewder than I was then; they asked me to be on another auxiliary. This move ensured that I would stay involved in church. Guest what? It worked!

In light of the fact that I could not just stop attending church, I prayed over and over to God, "Lord, if you are real, please reveal yourself to me." Well, God, the creator of the universe, answered my prayers.

On June 28, 1978, the Lord began the process of revealing Himself as my personal savior. He slowly began to answer the questions that had been troubling me. I received Christ under the leadership of Apostle Johnnie L. Washington of Tabernacle of Prayer.

In a quest to learn God's word, I enrolled in Bible School at the age of 14. The Bible School curriculum was designed for adults so the information was above my 14-year-old mind. I took classes like Christian Workers, General Bible 1 & 2, the Book of Hebrews, the Book of Acts, and the Book of Revelation. We had to learn scriptures verbatim, and I did very well at that. However, I still did not understand all the technical information about the types and shadows, the fig leaves, ram, Abraham being the father of many nations, and how we as Christians are grafted in. That was complex information for a young teen to grasp.

Now that I am older, I understand that Rev. Johnson and the Tabernacle of Prayer Bible Institute teachers were superlative in the education they provided, but I was just too young then to understand the relevance of what they taught to my daily life. From this understanding now as I look back, I vowed that I would use all my training to explain to others those things I did not understand at that young age. These were some of my questions:

1. If God is the God of Abraham, how can He be my God and my Heavenly Father?

2. Can God identify with me, the project life, and my struggles?

3. If God is good, why does life seem like a bad dream?

4. Why did my father abandon our family?

The *aim* of this book is to demonstrate the father nature of God in the context of families. The *objective* is to show you the unending love of our Heavenly Father through His covenants, dispensations, and the renowned patriarch families. The *purpose* is to demonstrate that a perfect God called imperfect fathers to preserve their families. The *goal* of this interactive book is to encourage individuals to enter into relationship with God and to see the relevance of the Bible in daily life. There are exercise questions to give you the opportunity to share a principle or something special that you have learned.

Let's start with looking at some important concepts before we go on this exciting journey of learning about "The Unending Love of a Father."

Let's champion for "whole families"!

What is a father? According to the dictionary, a father is a male person whose sperm unites with an egg resulting in the conception of a child. A father is in relation to his natural child or children. The word implies a clear connection to an offspring. The father/

male has an important role to play in the nurturing and development of his baby. It is the father who provides the scaffold for his family to develop their core values, beliefs, and actions. The scaffolding to build family empowers children to be confident in their place in their own family, in society, and in the world.

However, there is a problem in society that needs to be addressed. That problem is fatherlessness. "Fatherlessness," the Chairman of the National Initiative says, "is the engine that drives our most urgent social problems, from crime to adolescent pregnancy to domestic violence." In James 1:27 we are called upon to visit the fatherless and the widows in their afflictions.

According to statistics only 50% of children will spend their entire childhood in an **intact family**. For example, 24 million children in the U.S. live apart from their biological fathers. This problem is not just in the United States. It is universal. By the end of 2003, an estimated 143 million orphans (from all causes) ages 0-17 were reported in 93 developing countries.16.2 million of those children were double orphans having lost both parents according to *Orphan Statistics from Children on the Brink 2004*. As a result of these staggering numbers, many children, youth, and families fall prey to the following:

- Malnutrition, poverty, illiteracy

- Radical belief systems, human trafficking, sexual exploitation, illicit sexual behaviors

- Drugs, gangs, AIDS

- Hopelessness

Why are family development initiatives important?

This is what is important: God wants His children to pattern after His example in order to achieve *holistic development spiritually, emotionally, socially, financially, and physically.* The problem is that we have not followed His pattern, and the legacy of family is becoming endangered. This book is an interactive tool to give you life strategies to implement and apply in your daily lives to help return to the pattern of family.

With all due respect, sisters, please vow that you will forgive your father, grandfather, great-grandfather, brother, nephew, or uncle of any offenses and violations against you so that you can make better decisions in relationships pertaining to the opposite sex and break this cycle of fatherlessness.

The Relationship Circle

Relationship with God _____

Relationships are important. The relationship circle includes God, self, family, friends, systems, and nature. At the center of your world is your relationship with God. Life is good when you know your God and strive to make Him known. Our Heavenly Father is a relational God; therefore, when He created man, He created him to be relational. God wants to accomplish His work in the earth. He puts His mission and goal in the hearts of men to be the extension of Himself; however, no man is an island. So God chose to connect women and men to do His will to:

- carry out His mission, vision, and goals.
- embrace His loving kindness.
- receive His redemptive concern.
- rejoice in His nearness to His people.
- accept His faithful presence with His people.

Most people interact with other people, visit interesting places, and utilize material things in order to relate to one another. As said by Dr. John Townsend, "Relational supports should provide acceptance, understanding, feedback for growth, your personal Delta Force, normalization, wisdom, experiences, reality and perspective, and help you hold the line."

To repeat, the broad relational circle can be broken down into these six components: God, self, family, friends, systems, and nature. Let's look at each one individually.

1. Relationship between divine life (God) and human life

The Heavenly Father breathed an extension of Himself into you. In essence, He imparted life and breath to the first man, Adam. To this end, humankind is superior to any of God's other creations on earth. Humans are in a higher order and in a different category than the animals, birds, and sea creatures. God desires a relationship with you as He made you in His image.

2. Relationship with yourself

Your relationship with yourself is the second most important relationship that you can have. It involves your perception of yourself, how and what you think and feel about yourself. It is important to view yourself in a healthy light. The character, traits, attributes, disposition, and personality you develop work together to shape who you are. Your temperament is the inborn quality of yourself. It is the real you. Your soul is the essence of who you are. The soul consists of your mind, your will, and your emotions.

3. Relationship with family

An individual is a three part being: spirit, soul, and body. Individuals strive to live a balanced life in their careers, personal lives, and spiritual lives. Individuals make up families. Doctor Murray Bowen introduced the family systems theory. It has been suggested by Dr. Bowen that individuals cannot be understood in isolation from one another, but rather need to be understood as a part of their family since the family is an emotional unit.

What does family mean? Family is a group of relatives—a group of individuals who are closely related by birth, marriage, or adoption. Family is the most important institution in the world, and family life is an important social system. This family system includes any, some, or all of marriage, parenting, religion, culture, language, and tradition. God predetermined your lineage (your family before you), but the individuals in your family are responsible to leave a heritage or an inheritance for the next generations (your family after you). What is heritage? Heritage includes your birthright, family traditions, and customs. Building strong, healthy relationships within your family helps create strong, supportive families. Failure to build healthy relationships or creating poor or unhealthy relationships is very destructive to family life and to individuals in the family. Every family relationship is important.

Wellbeing is important for families to thrive. Wellbeing includes basic needs such as food, water, shelter, love, and even material things individuals and families want or desire. While food, water, and shelter are basic needs, love is also a true need. Material needs and wants range from small to large and can affect wellbeing by creating either harmony or disharmony. Keeping material wants in perspective and under control and providing first for true needs, including love in the relationships, is important for a strong family foundation.

4. Relationship with friends

A friend is a person attached to another person by feelings of affection or personal regard. Some friends are purpose-friends who can influence your life during good or bad times or through rich or poor times. They can give assistance or be a mentor. Some friends are in your life for a period of time and some are there for life. In essence, some relationships can have a long-lasting effect. To this end, it will take God to break the soul tie. The important thing is that with your true friends, you give and receive joy, love, and healthy support. Other people in your life — so-called friends — bring trouble, harm, and hurt. You need to protect yourself from those people in this category.

5. Relationship with systems

A system is a set of connected things or parts forming a complex whole. An agency, school, institution, or department would be examples of systems. No human being is completely self-reliant or self-sufficient. We have a deep longing to develop healthy interdependence with one another. Agencies or systems in our communities are examples of this interdependence. The goal is to enter into a mutually respectful and trusting relationship to accomplish or receive the system's benefit or mission on behalf of the individuals, couples, or families it serves. When we interact with these systems, it is a two-way relationship — a partnership between the person who has the need and the system delivering the benefit. This means an agency gives a benefit and the recipient is responsible to receive and put that benefit to good use.

For example, a school system delivers educational services. The benefit is education. Students should be responsible to study, take exams, and pass classes to receive the benefit of an education. Often the benefit of an education will help with getting a good job, contributing to family and society, and creating a meaningful life.

Systems in society are there to make society function smoothly, to help people live together in communities, large or small. They provide benefits like education, health care, and access to electricity, water, and trash pickup. They maintain streets, roads, and parks and provide other social assistance. You should receive services with appreciation and give back to the system by honorable and wise use of what they provide to make your life better. This allows you to be able to give back some measure of good to your own family and community.

6.   Relationship with nature/environment

The natural environment affects you and your family. We touched on the importance to receive, use wisely, and give back in discussing the relational part of the circle for systems. This cycle is especially true for the environment part of the relational circle. It is important for all of us to maintain a healthy relationship with the whole planet. This is where we live. We all (including you) need to take care of the earth. Each and everyone one of you have an important part to play in caring for this planet.

Regular daily care of your environment includes simple things like reusing, reducing, and recycling. For example, you can recycle garbage, cardboard, cans, tires, paper, trees, and wood, and thereby reduce waste in landfills and use less of nature's resources. By not polluting our earth, including our oceans, lakes, rivers, and streams, everyone can help keep the earth clean and beautiful.

Every little thing you do in your environment counts toward maintaining the earth or toward damaging the earth. Yes, air pollution can be reduced with responsible business practices, but you can do easier things like monitoring your car's emissions and driving fuel-efficient vehicles. Even simple things like not littering and not wasting water are helpful and important to protecting God's creation.

*Summary*_____

Take a few minutes and think about the concepts above and how the six components of the relational circle work together in your life — or should work together. Sometimes there are breakdowns. Sometimes connections don't get made. Sometimes things need to be fixed. How do we know what to do or where to start? As a good beginning, in this book we will be looking at the most important relationship, our relationship with our Heavenly Father, God.

PART I

OLD COVENANTS/THE COVENANTS WITH THE PATRIARCHS

≈∞≈

PROLOGUE

God Reveals Himself Through Covenants and Dispensations

The Bible gives a progressive picture of the people, places, and things that led to the events in the life of Christ. With this in mind, in order to rightly divide the Bible and to understand the introduction of Christ, we must study the Old Testament in light of the New Testament. It is through the covenants and dispensations that we see how the patriarchs of the Old Testament were a prelude to introducing Christ and the New Testament.

The book of Genesis was written by Moses around 1445-1405 B.C. The theme of Genesis is beginnings. The book is divided into two major parts. Chapters 1-11 provide an overview of human beginnings from Adam to Abraham. Chapters 12-50 record the beginning of the Hebrew people and focus on God's redemptive purpose through the lives of Israel's great patriarchs—Abraham, Issac, Jacob—and other leaders.

Let's take a journey to discover how the patriarchs were led by God to experience many cultures, backgrounds, ethnic groups, economic conditions, governments, and spiritual and religious groups on their journeys though life. All through the patriarchs' experiences, the underlying basis was a relational life with God. God's goal is for each man, family, and nation in the whole world to know the true and living God as Father and Savior. Today, God is searching for individuals to answer the call in order to establish His covenant, preserve families, and establish His Kingdom in the earth.

God's Master Plan _____

God's master plan in unfolding His character is to reveal what was concealed about Him in the scriptures.

The covenants and dispensations were mysteries to reveal the spiritual blessings of God to mankind. To paraphrase Ephesians 1:3-10, He chose us in Him before the creation of the world to be holy and blameless in His sight. This was done because it was His will. He took pleasure in adopting mankind as sons. He sealed the deal by redeeming us through His blood and forgiving us for our sins. This was all done according to the richness of God's grace. Eternal life is our new inheritance. With all wisdom and understanding, He made known to us the mystery of His will according to His good pleasure, which He purposed in Christ, to be put into effect when, in the dispensation of the fullness of times, He might gather us together in Christ — to bring unity to all things in heaven and on earth under Christ.

Paraphrasing Apostle Paul in Ephesians 3:2-5, he says: "You have heard of the dispensation of grace, which God has entrusted me to convey to you. It was by revelation that He revealed the mystery of Christ to me." This mystery wasn't revealed during earlier dispensations to the sons of men as it is now revealed to His apostles and prophets by the Spirit. The mystery is that the Gentiles are now to be fellow heirs with the Jews, members of the same body and share in the Divine promise of Christ by acceptance of the Gospel.

During the dispensation of grace or the church age, Christians are not required to live by the law. Those who accept Jesus as Savior are no longer under the bondage of sin. This new freedom doesn't give Christians a license to sin but rather to enter into a right relationship with the Heavenly Father and experience the good pleasures of God's will.

God used symbols, types, shadows, similes, metaphors, hyperbole, patterns, principles and methods, and means and ways to connect with humankind. Two of the many ways that God reveals Himself to men, women, and children are through covenants and dispensations.

God's Covenants _____

God wants to enter into a relationship with you and your family.
You may say that you do not believe that an angry God wants to enter into a relationship with you and your family. God chose to describe His relationship with His people through covenants. A *covenant* is a sovereign pronouncement by God where He establishes a relationship of responsibility. In essence, a *covenant*

is an agreement between two entities or people and involves promises on the part of each one to the other. The Bible uses the term *covenant* as an agreement between God and His people. Covenant is one of the central themes of the Bible. Jeremiah 34:18 records a covenant God made. Hebrew 13:20 reminds us of the eternal covenant that brought Jesus back from the dead.

There are two types of covenants: conditional covenants and unconditional covenants. A conditional covenant is bilateral: "If you will, then I will." The unconditional covenant is a unilateral covenant: "I will." There are eight covenants in the Bible: the Edenic, Adamic, Noahic, Abrahamic, Mosaic, Davidic, Palestinian, and the New Covenant. I will be speaking about each of them. Six are unconditional and two are conditional. The first three covenants are the Edenic, Adamic and Noahic covenants. These three covenants are universal and general to the whole of mankind. The Edenic and Mosaic covenants are the two conditional covenants God made. This means as people of God we have responsibilities to fulfill in these two covenants.

Dispensations of God _____

The second way God shows His characteristics is through dispensations.

A **dispensation** is a period of time, often called an "age," during which man is tested in respect to his obedience to some specific revelation of the will of God. There are seven dispensations: Innocence, Conscience or Moral Responsibility, Human Government, Promise, Law,

Church, and Kingdom. Note there are three important concepts that are implied in God's dispensations:

1. God makes deposits of divine revelation concerning God's will. His will is His word. His word embodies what God requires of man. It includes the duty and/or the conduct of man.

2. God gave man the stewardship of God's divine revelation. Man's responsibility is to obey God as Father. God chooses these tests of man's obedience for growth and development.

   Similarly, in order to experience developmental milestones, a new born baby must first go through the initial stages of development. It is during these stages that babies learn about themselves, the world, and limitations and abilities through trial and error. As newborn babies in Christ, we also learn through trial and error. As we experience these stages in life, we grow and develop through various experiences in Christ.

3. God created man with a God-shaped vacuum inside him that only God can fill. As a result, man has the capability to respond to God. Every human being interacts with God and the people of God. The intermingling of varied people, places, and things help us to grow and develop into healthy and productive members of society.

Entering a Relationship

Since covenants are about relationships and God's

dispensations are about how we respond to His testing in our relationship with Him, let's look once more at relationships.

Everyone would likely agree that relationships are challenging. In order to establish and maintain a healthy and vibrant relationship, both parties—employer/employee, father/family member, religious leaders/congregants, governments/citizens, member/group, organization/individual, God/man—must enter into a mutually respectful and trusting partnership.

The following principles will help you in all relationships. Using these simple measures will help you overcome responding negatively to button pushers and challenging personalities. It also is important to learn how to express your wants, needs, and desires so that you ensure that your needs are met in a balanced and wholesome manner. Here are Dr. Marshall Goldsmith's eight steps to achieve a *healthy and vibrant* relationship. This interpersonal skill set can be used in self, marital, business, and organizational relationship-building.

Dr. Marshall Goldsmith's
Interpersonal Skills Set

Step 1: *Ask yourself how you can be better*
Show respect, care, and concern for others around you; try to do what is right even when it isn't easy. This step encourages individuals to respond to others in a kind manner.

Step 2: *Listen*
Listen to what others have to say, be fully present when someone is talking to you. Listening helps the other person to be fully engaged in the conversation.

Step 3: *Reflect, think, and analyze*
Consider what you see, hear, speak, and think in light of your Christian faith and God's will. Self-reflection helps you to see what part you play in a relationship to build it up or to tear it down.

Step 4: *Say thanks often*
Express your gratitude to God and those around you.

Step 5: *Responses*
Act, speak, and think in ways that reflect God's characteristics. Responding appropriately helps you to control negative impulses and negative thoughts.

Step 6: *Be involved*
We are called to share God's will. Be involved in the process through your own right actions within the circle of relationships. Be concerned about those around you. Reach out, help, or just enjoy time together.

Step 7: *Change*

Change behaviors that are not pleasing to God. Those behaviors do not benefit you or those around you and only pull you away from obedience to God.

Step 8: *Follow up*

Stay in touch, be present in the lives of those around you, live up to commitments!

Making these skills a part of your everyday life and actions will help you become happier and more confident as your relationships strengthen and improve, within yourself, with those around you, and especially with God.

CHAPTER 1

Strategies to bring back the "fire" in your marriage
and strengthen your family

EDENIC COVENANT —
ADAM'S LIFE CLASSROOM

- **God made covenants with the patriarchs in order to show us how He wants us and our families to live in covenant relationship with Him.**

- **The 1st Covenant — Edenic (Genesis 2:16) — conditional covenant, test of obedience.**

- **The 1st Dispensation — Innocence (Genesis 1:28 and 3:6)**

Summary of the Covenants, Dispensations, and the Patriarchs: The Redemption Plan in Action

Adam was the father, the daddy, and the husband

God established an unending relationship with Adam and his descendants in the Garden of Eden. Adam was the first man God created. Adam was the first "patriarch." According to the Bible, Eden was located in Mesopotamia, probably in what is now modern southern Iraq near the Tigris and Euphrates flood plain, and was the beautiful place to live that God gave Adam.

With Adam's relationship to God, he had free access to God any time.

The Husband and Wife Relationship _____

The making of Adam

Genesis 1:27 reads: "God created man in His own image, in the image of God created He him: male and female created He them." God created man as spirit, soul, and body. Man is a spirit who has a soul and lives in a body (1 Thessalonians 5:23). God created two genders, male and female (Genesis 1:31 and Genesis 2:21). In Genesis 1:26–27, we see that the *Triune God* made a decision to create man in their image. Here we see the demonstration of an All Powerful God skipping over all the natural process of childbirth. Adam did not have a natural mother or father. Just as God is a triune being, God the Father, God the Son, and God the Holy Spirit, mankind is a triune being—mind, body, and spirit. When the Bible speaks of man being created in the image of God, man is like God. Further, it is on the basis of this image, men and women could respond to and have true fellowship with God. In addition, man possessed a moral likeness to God. For example, man was sinless; *Adam was created without sin*. Our conscience was given by God to be a moral compass.

The state of man

Man was hard wired to work and be productive from the beginning of his creation (Genesis 1:28-30). God gave Adam preeminence over the earth. God gave him the right to direct and govern the earth. As God-man,

Adam was equipped with supernatural wisdom. In other words, man was wired to run his home and the world. Likewise, the responsibility of caring, nurturing, guiding, disciplining, loving, providing for, and protecting a family is a weighty responsibility. God's providential care for Adam and Eve in Eden is a picture of how Adam is to provide for his family. Genesis 2:15 reads: "And the LORD God took the man, and put him into the Garden of Eden to dress it and to keep it."

If God had advertised the position for Adam in the "Garden Times," it would have read something like: "We are looking for a manager to oversee and tend to the daily operation of the garden. Job description: Excellent fishing, horticulture, and zoologist skills." Of course, I am kidding here, but God did create Adam and did give Adam the permission and responsibility to care for His garden world.

Man was wired to work
In Genesis 2:20, Adam named all the livestock, birds in the sky, and all the wild animals.

After Adam finished his first hard day at work, he did not have anyone to share his day with. God saw that Adam was lonely and had compassion so He created a *suitable helper* for Adam. In Genesis 1:28-30, God gave Adam a command to be fruitful and multiply. Adam could not populate the earth by himself. He needed a help-meet who was perfectly suitable for him. It takes two suitable persons to have a family, one male and one female. God's intent and requirement is that children be born inside holy matrimony. It takes two people of similar mindsets to raise a child in the way of the Lord.

Help-meet is a person who is working to produce a desired result. My brothers and sisters, Eve's role was to meet the holistic needs of her husband and children. In essence, she came alongside of Adam to assist with the health and wellbeing of their family.

God gave Adam a command

Did you know that humans were the first to possess a spirit so they would be able to communicate with and worship God? True love always requires choice. To this end, God wanted Adam to choose to love and trust Him. The only way to give this choice would be to forbid something and so give Adam a choice to obey or disobey—free will to choose.

Free will is the apparent ability to make choices free from certain kinds of constraints. Every human being is given free will. Adam, however, wasn't given a choice in the Garden of Eden. God did not give Adam a choice between eating from the tree of knowledge of good and evil and the tree of life. NO! He told Adam that he could eat from every tree in the garden EXCEPT from the tree of the knowledge of good and evil (Genesis 2:16-17). Eve wasn't formed yet. In essence, the command was given to Adam.

Man shares similar moral attributes of God

God is love, and God is good, merciful, gracious, compassionate, patient, truthful, faithful, and just. As we learn about the attributes of our Heavenly Father and his son, Jesus Christ, this knowledge empowers us to show those attributes to the world. Man was created with the capacity to be as Christ in the world (1 John 4:17).

God gives Adam a wife

God gave Adam a wife (Genesis 2:18) and responsibilities to care for his wife and family. Concerning the institution of marriage, God requires that a husband love his wife as Christ loves the church and gave Himself for the church. Remember, Eve was said to have been taken from Adam's flesh and bone in Genesis 2:21.

In the same way that Adam was responsible to care for Eve and their children, men, you are responsible for caring for your wife and children. Men are rugged by nature, but at your core, you have the capacity to love and honor your wives, and you can use your occupation or work to earn a living for your family.

The hierarchy of responsibility

Man must put God first, family second, church/religious affiliations third, and job/business fourth.

Different types of men

There are many types of men: the warrior-protector, the independent lone wolf, the adventurer, the wanderer, the traveler, the polite gentlemen, the civic-minded statesman, and the family man who loves his wife, children, and job. Also, there are the partiers, the players, the dreamers, and the sugar daddies. Men, think about which type of man you are

27

and ask yourself if you are living up to your true self. Make an effort to embrace these fundamental principles of manliness: courage, loyalty, integrity, resiliency, personal responsibility, and sacrifice.

As men, you are responsible for developing a mutual loving relationship with your spouse/significant other. Here are seven ways you can do this.

1. *Take care of your wife*
Provide for healthy foods, a decent house or apartment, and encourage her to take care of herself by exercising often and regularly visiting her doctor.

2. *Say thank you*
With the everyday stresses of work, home, and kids, it's easy to take your wife for granted. Whenever you feel the urge to criticize her, instead take the opportunity to say, "I appreciate you for being you!" Then help her out!

3. *Daily honeymoon*
Send love letters, massage her back, and rub her toes. Find out what she enjoys doing and do the things she likes, visit the places she enjoys, see the people she is excited to see. Go out on a date regularly, be the first to score a touchdown by complimenting her on what she is wearing or on her hairstyle, even if it is a weave or a hairstyle she always wears.

4. *Let her go out to play*
Girl time is important for women. Encourage her to have her play dates with the girls. Make a comfortable getaway spot at home so that she can get back in

balance after a long day at work, with the children, or doing community service.

5. *Make your wife a priority*
Make time for the two of you to connect on a regular basis. Let her know she's important to you. When there are heated discussions, put them behind you and start with a clean slate every day.

6. *Respect her and cherish her*
Don't belittle her, especially in front of others. Treat her like a queen, even when it is difficult to love her. If you keep treating her like a queen, she will begin to love herself and love you even more.

7. *Study your wife to understand her*
A female is a beautiful, interesting, and delicate creation of Almighty God. It is very important for a man to study his wife. Learn her temperament, personality, characteristics, and behavior. As a boyfriend/husband, you must be sensitive if your significant other has experienced a divorce, separation, incest, molestation, sexual assault, neglect, or physical or emotional abuse. Observe her moods, emotions, fears, procrastinations, and her quest to be perfect. Be helpful, not critical.

Do your best to provide a safe place for her to express herself through life's challenges. Do not trample over her to "push her buttons" or expose her weaknesses. Protect her by minimizing situations, images, people, places, and things that are triggers and stressors for her. Your role is to bring healing and wholeness to her so that you are her "superman." Help her so that the world can benefit from her life's contribution.

The making of Eve

In Genesis 2:21-23, we read that God put Adam asleep then He took one of Adam's ribs and made a woman. He brought the woman to Adam then Adam declared she was "bone of my bones and flesh of my flesh." The verses continue to explain she will be called "wo-man" because she was taken out of man.

God did not call man a dog, and He did not call the woman a female dog. When God completed all things, He looked at His creation and said that it was very good (Genesis 1:31).

The significance of Eve

Eve is the mother of all people and Adam's help-meet in the Garden.

While the traditional role of women has involved a caring nature and household-related work, it also has included positions such as teacher, accountant, data entry, receptionist, housekeeper, and nurse to name a few.

The contemporary role of women is much broader. Mae Carol Jemison, engineer, physician and NASA astronaut, was the first African American, female astronaut. Hillary Clinton ran for President of the United States. Madeline Albright, Condoleezza Rice, and Hillary Clinton have held the most senior cabinet position, Secretary of State, in the United States Government.

Women, whether you are in a traditional role or contemporary role, you as a married woman have the responsibility of developing a mutually loving relationship with your husband. Here are six ways to help do that.

1. *Take care of your husband*
Cook healthy foods, set aside money in your budget for his grooming, and ensure that he exercises regularly or plays a sport to help him stay healthy.

2. *Say thank you*
Whenever you feel the urge to complain, take the opportunity to say thank you instead! And if you cannot say anything good, take a deep breath or go for a long walk to avoid saying something that you will regret.

3. *Daily honeymoon*
Send love letters and let him eat sweets every now and then. Throw kisses at him and massage his back. Take him out on a date and compliment him even before he compliments you.

4. *Let him go out to play*
Guy time is important for men; let him have his time with the guys.

5. *Make your husband a priority*
With the everyday stresses of work, ministry, home, and kids, it's easy to take your husband for granted. Make time for the two of you to connect on a regular basis. Take an interest in his work and hobbies. Let him know he's important to you.

6.   *Love and respect him*

Don't disrespect him publically or privately. Treat him like a king even if he doesn't deserve to be treated like a king. If you continue to treat him like a king, he might start to act like a king!

Keeping the "In-laws" out

A man is required to leave his father and mother and cleave to his wife (Genesis 2:24-25). As a result of the man leaving his father and mother, he and his wife become one flesh. This is the season that husbands and wives begin to create a home of their own, independent of their parents. Both learn through trial and error how to prepare their favorite meals, make a budget, raise children, entertain wholesome company, and share duties for the upkeep of the home. They learn how to balance work, child rearing, play, and family life while being responsible and loyal to each other.

Now let's look at the hierarchy of a family

Adam was formed first, then Eve. Because of the creation order of man, God ordained that men be the head (1 Timothy 2:13). Thus, man is the spiritual leader of the home. Let's look at the analogy. The head has eyes, mouth, nose, and ears. The man has the following responsibilities.

Man is the head of the family

The father is to **see** and have *insight* for good company for his children, make good judgment calls in family life and business life, and develop a keen insight to discern evil predators. He is to be a visionary for the home, community, church, and world. As the head of the family, the father **declares** life over his family and extended family. A father should **listen, discern,** and **hear** as well as speak words. A father can **sense** impending trouble on the horizon and put strategies in place to avert it.

The First Family _____

What is the meaning of family?

Hospital nurseries do not have to identify fathers on the baby's identification card. I know that while the identification of the father may cause legal issues for some, it is a privilege for others. In the words of Mr. Johnny L. Johnson, Jr., MBA, "... man is father, daddy, and the husband in families." A family is a group of people living together and functioning as a single household, usually consisting of parents and their children. For example, a family is made up of a father, mother, and a child or children. Also, family includes an extended group of people who are closely related by birth, marriage, or adoption.

Parenting skills

To reiterate, God is revealed as a Relational Being who created Adam and Eve so that He could have a loving, nurturing, and caring relationship throughout eternity. The miracle of this intimate fellowship is that God's image is seen in our lives as we reflect God's love, glory, and holiness.

The characteristics of God were required to be exemplified in Adam's personal and public life.

Adam and Eve consummated their marriage, and Cain and then later Abel were born. Adam had the capacity to love his children by doing the following: providing comfort, protection, nurture, love, food, shelter, clothing, identity, and security. These are some of the ingredients that make children feel loved, safe, confident, and secure.

With respect, fathers, you have been given the responsibility to nurture your children. It begins before birth in order that they can become healthy holistically in mind, body, and spirit as they grow into adults. This can be challenging if you are not married to your child's mother or if you are divorced, separated, or have a blended family or if you are serving in the armed forces, work long hours, or live in a different city or town. It is even more difficult when your situation involves harmful things like involvement with illegal drugs, or if you are incarcerated or have a restraining order against you. I submit, fathers, you must find a way to be in your child's life. I encourage you, fathers, make it happen to help your child or children.

Here are two helpful resources:

- The National Fatherhood Initiative: 301-948-0599

- The American Association for Marriage and Family Therapy: 703-838-9808

ADAMIC COVENANT
(Adam's Life Classroom Continues)

- **Humankind enters a state of Moral Responsibility**

- **The 2nd Covenant — Adamic (Genesis 3:15) — conditional covenant**

- **The 2nd Dispensation — Conscience or Moral Responsibility (Genesis 3:7 and Genesis 4:1-8:14)**

Lucifer and the 3rd host of the angelic beings were cast out of heaven (Isaiah 14:12, Luke 10:18, Hebrews 12:22 and Revelation 9:1 and 12:4). Lucifer needed a body in order to promote his kingdom and mission in the earth. With this in mind, Lucifer, also called Satan, entered into a serpent and used the serpent's words to beguile Eve, the wife of Adam, to disobey God (Genesis 3:14). As a result, Eve shares the forbidden fruit with her husband, Adam, and consequently, he disobeys God's command. Subsequently, the human race lost its right-standing with God (Romans 5:12). The serpent was beautiful and the most subtle of creatures. God and Jesus both cursed the serpent. The result was that the serpent would be on his belly and eat dust all the days of its life and be at enmity with women. Take care not to be a tool of Satan or allow him to speak through you to entice and beguile someone to disobey God.

Before the fall of mankind, physically man would have lived forever and Eve was on the same level as Adam. With the fall of mankind, the relationship of mankind to God and to creation changed. There was eternal separation from God (Genesis 2:16-17) and physical death. Now Eve is to be ruled by her husband and experience extreme pain and sorrow during childbirth. God did not curse Adam, but God did curse the ground to make Adam (mankind) have to work to care for self and family. Family life was turned upside down. Adam blamed God, and Eve blamed the serpent. This began the blame game. But it's not a game! God also gave a promise of the redeemer (Genesis 3:15-16) to bring mankind back to God.

Adam represents mankind as a whole. After Adam came the generations and the generations' life cycles as mentioned in Genesis 5:1.

According to the Bible, a generation is 40, 70, or 100 years. In essence, a new generation begins at the birth of your son (See Genesis 15:16, 21:5). Seventy years is a generation according to the average age of man at his death in Psalms 90:10.

Today we can expect life expectancy beyond 70 years old, but it is not the number of years that is important. The important thing is to live and love life as a gift from God to do His work. It doesn't matter what generation you are born in or what the "powers that be" may call you, it is up to you to fulfill your God-given destiny and reach your full potential to forge a path for the next generation. "Are you a covenant generation or are you a cursed generation?" becomes the question (Genesis chapter 4).

What can we learn from Adam's generation? _____

Romans 5:12 tells us that through one man sin entered the world and therefore everyone that was born after Adam was born into sin. Jesus is the second Adam. By His obedience, the world will be made righteous.

Sin and a negative pattern of behavior don't have to go from one generation to the next. You do not have to believe the erroneous theology that you are cursed. Exercise your God-given right (your free will) to choose between good and evil and break any negative cycle in your family line!

Fratricide is the act of a person who kills their brother. Sibling rivalry is jealous competition between siblings. _____

Adam's sin influenced his family. Cain and Abel were the sons of Adam. Cain was a farmer and Abel was a shepherd. Cain brought a fruit offering to the LORD, and Abel brought the first sheep from his flock. The LORD accepted Abel's offering and rejected Cain's. Afterwards Cain was angry so the LORD told him that if he just did what was right, he would be accepted, but if he did not, then "sin [would be] at the foot of his door." Cain did not release his anger. Instead Cain killed his brother Abel in the first recorded murder (Genesis 4:1-15). Cain killed his own brother due to unchecked anger, resentment, and jealousy.

In Genesis 4:10 when the LORD asked Cain about

his brother's whereabouts, Cain responded, "I do not know! Am I responsible to watch over and defend my brother from harm?" Then the LORD cursed Cain, making it so that Cain's harvest would not be as fertile. Cain became a wanderer. The LORD placed a mark on Cain's forehead to keep people from killing him. The LORD's forgiveness is demonstrated when he told Cain sevenfold vengeance would come upon anyone who took Cain's life.

Why did God reject Cain's offering? Maybe it was because the ground was cursed in Genesis 3:17. Or maybe it was because Cain did not honor God by offering the best of his first crop.

Poor Eve was left grieving because she lost two sons.

Everyone has the ability to choose between right and wrong _____

Enoch is Cain's son and Adam's grandson. Enoch was notably a righteous individual who promoted morality and values in a society that had gone wild (Genesis 5:22, 24). He broke the generation cycle of his family.

In contrast, Lamech, the 5 times grandson of Cain, was a polygamist and a murderer (Genesis 4:18-24). Lamech was Noah's father. Noah did not let his father's lifestyle dictate his lifestyle. Noah was a man of integrity, and he walked maturely in his generation (Genesis chapter 5). Noah did not have a lot of role models in his family except for Enoch, Methuselah, Meth, and Seth.

Today psychologists tell us individuals are influenced by the behavior of their parents and family members. This is why mentoring, coaching, and community programs are important. They provide positive role models for young men growing up without their father. The role models help them develop awareness of their thinking, feelings, and actions. The role models can help those they are mentoring or coaching to identify their positive core values and beliefs. Through their mentoring, they help youth become empowered to self-regulate and self-manage. This kind of positive mentoring helps our males graduate high school, graduate from a trade school/college, wed, embrace family life, business, ministry, and involvement in community services. They disdain depravity, sexual immorality, violence, and murder, which plague our families today.

Does God punish children for their parent's sin? Deuteronomy 24:16 says that "fathers shall not be put to death for their children, nor children put to death for their fathers; each is to die for his own sin." You can read more about this in Deuteronomy 20:5-6, Ezekiel 18:20, Jeremiah 31:29-30, and Matthew 23:35.

Chapter 1 — Questions to extend learning

According to the roles and responsibilities of Adam and Eve, describe how can you strengthen your family and enhance your relationship with your family.

_____

_____

_____

_____

_____

_____

What are your personality traits and how do they affect your family leadership style?

_____

_____

_____

_____

_____

_____

CHAPTER 2

**A good father made bad mistakes yet
God gave him grace**

NOAHIC COVENANT —
NOAH'S LIFE CLASSROOM

- God initiated the promise "I will be with you and I will be a God to you" (Genesis 17:7-8). Matthew 24:37 declares: "But as the days of Noah were, so shall also the coming of the Son of man be."

- The 3rd Covenant — Noahic Covenant (Genesis 9:9, 11, 16) — unconditional covenant

- The 3rd Dispensation — Human Government (Genesis 8:15 and 8:16-11:32)

The question before us is: "What was it like during the days of Noah?" In Noah's day, God offered repentant generations His forgiveness and an opportunity to start over. Wake up, fathers! Jesus is giving you a fresh start so that you can save your family.

The state of humankind today is parallel to the conditions before the flood. In the 21st century, the Northern, Southern, Eastern and Western hemispheres are experiencing record breaking earthquakes, floods, tsunamis, snowstorms, blizzards, as well as suicides, murders, attacks on the unborn, domestic and international terrorism, social issues, political upheavals, spiritual apostasy, bondage, sexual slavery, human trafficking, hatred, hunger, pain, depression, oppression, bitterness, and sickness.

There are people who are unaware of these conditions. There are those who see them and conscientiously care for humanity. And unfortunately, there are those who are selfish and do nothing. Similarly, in the Old Testament times, people did not heed warnings about the times or pay attention to the catastrophic events that were taking place. They did not prepare themselves for the impending flood but were partying, swapping spouses, divorcing, and doing evil. The good news for today is that just as God gave Noah a plan to save the world and especially his family, God will give you a plan to preserve your children, grandchildren, and great grandchildren.

Two primary ways sin was manifested before the flood: sexual lust and violence

Unrestrained Sensual Lust means having uncontrolled desire for a person or thing. Genesis 6:2-4 tells that the sons of God saw that the daughters of men were fair (pretty). The Sons of God had sex with the daughters of men and produced children. The sons of God were probably the descendants of Seth or fallen angels who intermarried with the daughters of men. Some of the women may have been women from the family of Cain. According to the Bible, Cain's family was ungodly.

Also before the flood, sin was manifested in

Unrestrained Violence. Adam's son Cain killed his brother Able (Genesis 4:8). Methuselah's son Lamech killed a young man (Genesis 4:23).

Why did God destroy the earth? Where does sin begin?

Genesis 6:5 recounts that God saw that the wickedness of mankind was great in the earth and that every *imagination of their thoughts of their hearts* was continually only evil. This scripture suggests that our hearts can think or imagine good or bad thoughts. This is why mankind must be born again. When you are born again, you go through a process of having your mind renewed by the word of God. The Holy Spirit empowers you to cast down every high thought that is contrary to the knowledge of God (Romans 12:1).

Fear, powerlessness, hatred, jealousy, envy, and malice are seated in our emotions. These inordinate passions are matters of the heart; they start out as a seed and, if left unchecked, will grow into a strong, poisonous tree. To paraphrase Matthew 15:18, what comes out of the mouth proceeds from the heart, and this defiles a person (New American Bible). The Bible surmises that the heart gives birth to evil thoughts, murders, adulteries, fornication, thefts, false witness, and blasphemies.

Dealing with unresolved anger _____

The Bible says go to your brother while he is with you when you have unresolved anger or negative feelings in your heart. You must go to your brother, sister, co-worker, supervisor, pastor, priest, nun, minister, imam, rabbi, political representative, teacher, or neighbor and clear the air by addressing the "big elephant" in your heart. Now I know that there are times that you have to wait to address an angry and irrational person, but most of the time, you can speak to the individual right away. If you intentionally keep feeding the negative emotions, you open the door for a spirit of fear, insecurity, hopelessness, cowardliness, rage, covertness, competition, perverted sexual sin, conniving behavior, or violence to enter you. These unresolved feelings can result in an individual murdering another person with what comes out of his mouth or by literally taking someone's life.

*How did God respond to the sinful state of man on the earth?*_____

Genesis 6:6-7 reveals God as a God who can feel regret and grief. God said, "I regret creating man and my spirit will not always strive with man, he is flesh." Although Our Heavenly Father is loving, merciful, and long-suffering, He is about to display His judgment on the human race. So He concludes, "I will destroy man whom I have created from the face of the earth: both man and beast and the creeping things and the fowls of the air; for it repented me that I have made them."

Noah had a personal relationship with God _____

More specifically, the scripture declares that Noah walked with God (Genesis 3:9). This means that Noah followed in the steps of God's will. He cooperated with the intimate relationship that God initiated with Adam in Genesis 3:8. Note, it is God who takes the lead in establishing, maintaining, and restoring a healthy relationship with his people. Because of God's relationship with Noah, Noah found grace in the eyes of the LORD (Genesis 6:8). Please take note that this is the first time that the word grace appears in the Bible. Here the word grace is translated as favor. In other words, God's thoughts toward Noah were favorable, charitable, and hospitable.

A new beginning _____

The Bible declares that there is nothing new under the sun. Noah lived during a time of human depravity that manifested itself in sex outside the context of marriage and senseless and blatant violence. The life style sounds like today. But Noah conducted himself in a holy manner. He was a righteous man who feared God, so God called Noah for a special assignment. His assignment was to build an ark, warn people about the coming catastrophic judgment, and tell them about the new beginning on earth.

Our lesson from this is that although grace is undeserved and unearned, be conscientious and be as intentional as Noah to follow God's word, and you will find grace in God's eyes.

The instructions, the ark, and the flood ("Let's build something ...") _____

Genesis 6:14-20 tells about Noah and the ark.

Paraphrasing the account, God tells Noah to take the instructions He gave him and follow them to the letter. Noah was to build the ark to God's specifications using durable gopher wood. God told him to include rooms, windows, and a door on the side of the ark. The ark was to have lower, second, and third stories. He told Noah to gather two of every type of every flesh that has the breath of life. More specifically, gather the male and female of the fowl, cattle, and creeping things on the earth so that they can repopulate the earth. He also told Noah to build a place to store food for him, his family, and the animals. And Noah did as God instructed.

Although Noah never saw it rain on the earth for 40 days and 40 nights, he heard the rain. Noah listened and followed the instructions from God (Genesis 6:19-22 and Genesis 7) and so he and his family were saved.

Focal point _____

Our Heavenly Father is intrinsically loving, merciful, and longsuffering. Through His covenant, God vowed that He would rescue all who would come into the ark and specifically that He would keep Noah and his family safe throughout the torrential flood.

God cares about your spiritual, physical, social, emotional, financial, and mental well-being. His judgment cleansed the earth of the extreme corruption of men and women in order to introduce a new relationship with God for the human race.

Why were the floodwaters significant? _____

According to 1 Peter 3:21, the ark represented protection from judgment and the floodwaters represented the cleansing blood of Jesus. The flood is symbolic of souls being saved by water; however, water baptism apart from Jesus's blood doesn't put away the filth of the flesh.

The covenant with Noah in Genesis 6:18 reads: "With thee will I establish my covenant; and thou shalt come into the ark, thou, and thy sons and thy wife, and thy sons' wives with thee."

The flood took place during the second dispensation. Noah and his family left the ark after the third dispensation. You can read this account in Genesis 8:15-11:32.

Application _____

At the age of 600, Noah had audacious faith in God, prepared the ark, and warned the unbelievers about the impending flood. Hebrews 11:7 tells us that today, we are called to intercede and stand in the gap for all the families of the earth. More specifically, we must strategically build God's church, build individuals and families, and warn the unsaved of judgment from fire at the end of time. Also, we must empower believers to live victorious lives in the earth and encourage the unbeliever to turn to the true and living God like Noah, who got instructions from God, looked at the probability of a flood, and yet was moved by faith to follow God's instructions.

I encourage you — hear the instructions God is giving you for your life and your family's life. Do not live your life based on history, but live by faith and walk in the spirit to accomplish all that God has instructed you.

What is the purpose of capital punishment? _____

When He saw the unrestrained and senseless violence in the human race, God regretted that He made man. In an effort to guard the sanctity of life, God instituted another part to this covenant. Genesis 9:6 says: "whoso sheds man's blood, by man his blood shall be shed; for in the image of God made He man." He was referring to capital punishment.

God's Covenant of no more floods _____

The Noahic covenant was instituted centuries before the time of Abraham. God made an unconditional covenant with Noah. It starts in Genesis 9:8-10. God demonstrated his love to Noah and Noah's sons by the following statements: "And God spoke unto Noah, and to his sons with him, saying, And I, behold I establish my covenant with you and with your seed after you. And with every living creature that is with you, of the fowl, of the cattle, and of every beast of the earth with you: from all that go out of the ark, to every beast of the earth." God made this covenant to Noah and his descendants and extended it to all Noah's livestock and all that he had in his possession.

The Noahic covenant made with Noah in Genesis 9:11 reads: "And I will establish my covenant with you: neither shall all flesh be cut off any more by the waters of a flood; neither shall there anymore be a flood to destroy the earth."

God's covenant with Noah was monergistic, which means that it is a "One Worker" covenant. God provided the covenant and God carried it out. His later covenant with Abraham was also monergistic. This is good news to the human race!

Covenant of God's mercy and faithfulness to His word ("... a rainbow in the cloud") _____

After God made the awesome covenant with Noah that He would never again destroy the world by flood, He gave Noah a sign and reminder of His promise. He set a rainbow in the cloud as a token of His covenant (Genesis 9:12-17). The beautiful colors of the rainbow are red, orange, yellow, green, blue, indigo and violet.

Noah was a good provider but he developed a drinking problem and neglected his responsibilities _____

Noah had three sons, Shem, Ham, and Japheth. To support his family, Noah became a farmer, and he planted a vineyard. Noah took advantage of his fruit producing farm and made wine from his grapes. Unfortunately, Noah drank so much wine that he took off all his clothes then passed out. His son Ham saw that his father was naked and ran and told his two brothers. Shem and Japheth took a garment and walked backwards so as to avoid seeing their father's "birthday suit," and they covered their father's nakedness (Genesis 9:18-23). When Noah woke up from his drunken stupor, he knew that Ham had seen him naked.

Noah pronounces a curse on his grandson Canaan __

Noah's alcohol level impeded his judgment to the point that he pronounced a curse on Canaan who was Ham's son and Noah's grandson. Noah did not curse Ham. Genesis 9:24-27 records the two-prong curse and blessing, which was that Ham's son Canaan was to become a servant (slave) of Ham's brothers Shem and Japheth and that God would prosper Japheth.

Abuse of drugs and alcohol causes trouble in your relationships ____

The point I want to convey is that Noah should not have gotten drunk, naked, and lost consciousness. During his drunken stupor, his family was vulnerable to predators, home invaders, abuse, and neglect. Then when Noah awoke, he cursed Ham through Ham's son Canaan.

Why would a father curse his grandson, his own flesh and blood? Noah could have been traumatized by the fact that most of his friends, neighbors, extended relatives, and most of humanity died in the flood. Further, we do not know the intent of Ham's action. However, we could infer that Ham was in shock about seeing his father naked, or perhaps he was out to show his father's indiscretions. Nonetheless, Noah's punishment of his son Ham did not fit his son's offense.

Staying in balance _____

Fathers, mothers, leaders, all of us — it is wise to stay in balance or get back in balance immediately after you engage in a demanding event or project. Because of our human frailty, the likelihood of becoming susceptible to temptations and indiscretions increases when we are out of balance. Think about what happened to Noah, the preserver of his family, when he fell out of balance and what effect such behavior has on humanity today.

Today, according to the National Institute on Alcohol Abuse and Alcoholism, approximately 7.2 percent or 17 million adults in the United States ages 18 and older received the medical diagnosis of "alcohol use disorder" (AUD) in 2012. Specifically, 11.2 million men and 5.7 million women were diagnosed with an alcohol disorder. It is estimated 855,000 adolescents, ages 12-17, had an AUD that year.

Are you dependent on alcohol, illegal drugs, or prescription medication such as beer, wine, or liquor, marijuana, meth, designer drugs, heroin, cocaine or morphine, oxycodone or other medications? Have your children become terrified of you because of your dependency on one or more of these drugs? Do you regret literally cursing at your children or sexually assaulting them because you were intoxicated? Do you have a drinking problem? Are you drinking more and more to get the effect you want? Have you tried to stop and couldn't? Are you sick and tired of being sick? Is your drinking causing chaos and abuse in your family? Do you become belligerent and abusive to your family while drinking? If you answered yes to any of these questions, please use the SAMHSA Treatment Locator 1-800-662-4357 or call the National Institute on Drug Abuse 1-877-643-2644 to get help.

Humanity's global hustle _____

Many people throughout the world use this scripture where Noah cursed Ham's son Canaan to justify their practice of slavery. For the record, the practice of slavery in any form goes against principles of God's Covenant. Our Heavenly Father's Covenant promotes health and wellbeing for all the families of the earth. God's intent was for all mankind to be free—including free of slavery. The system of slavery was instituted by mankind, not God.

What is slavery? _____

Slavery is a legally recognized system in which people are considered the property or chattel of another. Slavery is when a human being owns another human being. It involves the selling of men, women, boys, and girls for monetary, sexual, and/or domestic gain. Around 1400-1600 A.D., humanity (Asia, Africa, Australia, Europe, North America, and South America) profited monetarily from slavery. According to "Slavery in America Black History," "It is said that slavery in American began when the first African slaves were brought to the North American colony of Jamestown, Virginia, in 1619 to aid in the production of such lucrative crops as tobacco." Also, Spanish traders began to bring slaves from Africa to Spain. In addition, as Portugal increased its presence along China's coast, they began trading in slaves. Other ethnic groups were enslaved as well.

The negative effects of slavery were generational___

Whole parts of the population didn't obtain human rights in the United States until around 1960. They were held down on the "food chain" and kept out of the mainstream professions. They were brainwashed, abused, maimed, and tortured—mentally, physically, spiritually, relationally, emotionally, financially, and socially. They experienced extreme prejudice and suffered from racism. They were ostracized by other ethnic groups and separated from their siblings, families, tribes, and nations. In the 21th Century, it is said that the United States Penal system is the "Modern Day Slavery."

Slavery occurred in other ways as well. During the first dispensation of law, we see laws concerning slavery. Provisions were made for the freeing of slaves. A case-in-point for this would happen during the year of jubilee. During the year of jubilee, slaves were released and reunited with their families. In spite of the declaration of human rights, man's quest is to ensure that slavery is perpetuated in one form or another.

Brothers/fathers and leaders, let the Spirit of God free you to set others free so that they can reach their full potential. You do not have to follow in the footsteps of the males in your family, community, or the world.

If you are holding anyone against their will, release them now. More importantly, free yourself from these destructive behaviors such as hatred, malice, jealousy, bitterness, retribution, sexual perversion, drunkenness, and womanizing. Stop and allow God to transform your mind. Get counseling and be determined to change for yourself and the sake of your family.

We are all part of the human race _____

The generations of Noah through his three sons Shem, Ham, and Japheth increased as told in Genesis chapter 10.

Ham's descendants went to southern Arabia, southern Egypt, the east shore of the Mediterranean, and north coast of Africa.

Canaan's descendants made their home in Canaan. The borders of the Canaanites were from Sidon, Gerar, Gaza to Sodom and Gomorrah to Admah, Zeboim, and Lasha. Canaan was the grandson cursed by Noah. The land of Canaan later became the home of the Jewish people.

I had to do further research because the footnotes in my Bible said Canaan's descendants were not black, however, in Genesis 10:6, the Bible affirms that Canaan's brothers were Cush (Ethopia), Mizraim (Egypt), and Phut (Libya). According to Race and History Forum, the Canaanites were white people. Note: The oldest *Homo sapiens* (human) remains discovered to date were found in Africa (Ethopia).

Japheth's descendants were the Medes, Greeks, and Caucasians of Europe and Asia who travelled north and settled near the coastlands of the Black Sea and Caspian Sea (Genesis 10:2-5).

Shem's descendants were the Jews, Assyrians, Syrians and Elamites who settled in Arabia and the Middle East Valley (Genesis 10:21-31).

Chapter 2 — Questions to extend learning

Are you a good role model for your family? If so, describe two ways you keep your family from engaging in violence, sexual immorality, anger, hatred, and selfishness.

_____

_____

_____

_____

_____

_____

Have you ever gotten drunk or so high that you were not aware of your surroundings? Have you neglected the welfare of your children? If so, please describe how you plan to get help and prevent this from happening again. Noah got drunk and there were terrible consequences. Learn from his lesson. Do some soul searching to determine if you have been intoxicated while at work, ministry, school, community service, or with your guy friends or your girlfriends.

_____

_____

_____

_____

_____

_____

CHAPTER 3

Breaking unwanted cycles in your family

THE ABRAHAMIC COVENANT — ABRAHAM'S LIFE CLASSROOM

- **The 4th Covenant — Abrahamic (Genesis 12:2) — unconditional covenant**

- **The 4th Dispensation — Promise (Genesis 12:1 — Exodus 18:27)**

- **A perfect God chooses imperfect men to show His perfect love.**

Fathers are called to take the spiritual leadership in the home. Fathers, your thoughts, decisions, and actions can create a pattern of behavior for your family. Be careful what pattern you provide. "And, ye fathers, provoke not your children to wrath: but bring them up in the nurture and admonition of the Lord" (Ephesians 6:4).

The power of one

In this chapter, we will learn how God revealed Himself to Abram and his descendants. The promise was given that this one man, Abraham, would have a son, (Isaac), who in turn would become a family (Jacob and Esau), and out of this family, a nation would come forth (Jacob). And out of this nation would come a family of nations. Jacob's 12 sons formed the 12 tribes of the Israelites. More importantly, out of this nation Jesus

Christ, the Son of the Living God, would be born, placing Jesus from the seed that would come forth from the generation of Abram who became Abraham. Note: God also promised to bless and multiply Ishmael as well. You will read this later in the chapter.

The promise of this covenant is to all who would accept Jesus. "And if you are in Christ, then you are Abraham's seed, and heirs according to the promise" (Galatians 3:16, 28-29) and again in Ephesians 3:5-6, "Gentiles have become fellow heirs." Romans 11:13-27 says: "God grafts all who believe in Him into the family of Abraham." So, all believers without regard to race or culture can be grafted in as God's people through belief in Jesus Christ.

With all due respect to God's chosen people _____

It doesn't matter which nation or culture the children of Israel came from; the fact of the matter is Jesus could have come have through any culture. For example, He could have come from the African culture, Asian, Australian, European, North American, or South American culture. Jesus's coming through the children of Israel was according to God's providence. This doesn't make the Jews above any other ethnic groups. Jesus transcends culture, background, and ethnicity; He isn't limited by ethnicity. He brings all believers together.

Separation for preparation _____

The promises are first recorded in Genesis 12:1-3: "The LORD had said unto Abram, 'Get thee out of thy country, and from thy kindred, and from thy father's house, unto a land that I will show thee: and I will make of thee a great nation, and I will bless thee and make thy name great; and thou shalt be a blessing: And I will bless them that bless thee, and curse him that curse thee: and in thee shall all families of the earth be blessed.'"

Remember, a dispensation is a period of time during which man is tested in respect to his obedience to some specific revelation of the will of God. Abram had to get a new perspective about his family, friends, and relatives, as well as his culture, beliefs, background, status, and mindset. God's covenant of promise to Abram was based on trust. As a result of Abram's obedience, his son and his grandson would experience the blessings of God.

Do you wonder how you can identify with this Jewish family? Jesus is the incorruptible seed that came down through the line of Abraham to redeem Israel and the Gentiles. Genesis 3:15 and 17:1-6 affirm Jesus is the promised seed. Those who believe in Jesus's work on the cross of Calvary come from the incorruptible seed of Christ. 1 Peter 1:23 states: "For you have been born again, not of the corruptible seed, but of incorruptible, by the word of God, which live and abide forever. Those who believe are now of Christ's family." Galatians 3:29 says: "And if ye be Christ's, then are ye Abraham's seed, and heirs according to the promise." God wanted Abraham and his generations, all the way to your family, to walk by faith and live in the promised land.

The promise of land represents the heavenly land for all those who are heirs of Abraham, which benefits Africans, Asians, Australians, Europeans, North Americans, and South Americans — believers from anywhere in the world. The invitation of salvation has been extended to the world. Galatians 3:8 reads: "And the scripture foreseeing that God would justify the heathens through faith, preached before the gospel unto Abraham, saying, in thee shall all nations be blessed."

We no longer have to live by the law because now we receive God's grace. Now that faith is come, we are to receive justification only through faith in Jesus Christ. God wants to cause a paradigm shift in our mindset about our belief system, background, and culture. We are all called to walk by faith. Galatians 3:11 declares: "But that no man is justified by the law in the sight of God." The Greek and Hebrew words for "law" (*nomos* and *torah* respectively) mean "teaching" or "direction." The law can refer to the Ten Commandments, the Pentateuch, or any commandment in the Old Testament. This includes the sacrificial system of the Mosaic covenant.

Paul said in Galatians 3:12 that "the law is not of faith: but, the man that doeth them shall live in them." In Galatians 3:7, Paul said, "know you therefore that they which are of faith, the same are the children of Abraham." In other words, those of faith have the same inheritance and promises as the children of Abraham.

Because of the ongoing and universal oppression of the dark skinned people, you may reject the

Bible because you believe that it was written by the light-skinned man. Please read and pray about God revealing this scripture to you. Galatians 3:6 affirms: "…Abraham believed God, and it was accounted to him as righteousness." Similarly, as Abraham's faith is synonymous to Christ's righteousness, so your faith is equal to Christ's righteousness. Further, the word of God contained in the Holy Bible must be mixed with saving faith. It is for you to experience salvation for you and your household.

Tragedy comes even to the chosen family _____

Genesis 11 tells that Abram was from Ur of the Chaldees (Mesopotamia). This ancient city was located about 100 miles southeast of Babylon near the Euphrates River, in what is now known as Iraq. Soon tragedy struck Abram's family. His brother Haran died in Ur of the Chaldees (Genesis 11:28-32). His father Terah was still living. Many believe that there isn't any other loss and grief more traumatic than the death of a child. This disrupts the order of life. I cannot image the grief that Terah was going through. After the untimely death of Abram's brother Haran, the family travelled toward Canaan to the city of Haran. Its ruins lie within present-day Southern Turkey in upper Mesopotamia. After their migration, death came to the family once again. Terah died in Haran at the age of 205 (Genesis 11:32).

Separation from his kindred (family) _____

At the age of 75, Abram received a call from God to

go to an unknown land, which God promised to reveal to Abram. The first prong of the instruction was to separate Abram from his father and his country. This call came after Terah had just moved Abram and this family from Ur of the Chaldees to Haran. The stop at Haran was temporary. Nahor and Milcah also settled in Haran along with Terah. Let's keep track of the family. Nahor was Terah's son and Milcah was Terah's grandson (Genesis 11:31).

Leave his father's house _____

God called Abram while he was living in Haran among extended family to leave the country (Genesis 12:1). His father represented his old associations. God told Abram He would show him the country that he was to move to. The strange thing about this separation is that God did not tell Abram the exact "city, state, and zip code" or even country that he was to travel to. Abram had to take steps of faith and trust in God. Further, this guidance turned out to be a progressive movement toward the promise land. This had to be unsettling to say the least. Yet Abram obeyed and took his family, including his nephew Lot, onward to Canaan.

An imperfect father and family _____

Now that Abram was onboard, let's think about Sarai's thoughts on this matter. I can just imagine the conversation with his wife, "Ah, baby, we are going to relocate again." Sarai says, "Oh dear, that sounds great! Where are we going to relocate?" Abraham might have replied, "Ah, ah, God did not tell me. Honey, you are going to have to trust me on this one!" Sarai might have retorted something like, "Here you go again on your journey of adventures to 'nowhere,' and you want me to trust you!" Sarai might have thought, "There he goes, chasing wild dreams of a better life." But she went with him.

*Men, protect your wives*_____

We see Abram denying that Sarai was his wife on two occasions. In Genesis 12:10-20 and Genesis 20. In the first denial in Genesis 12:10-20, we see Abram travelling from east of Bethel on his way to the Land of Canaan. But Bethel was experiencing a famine, so Abram migrated to Egypt to escape the famine. (A famine is a widespread scarcity of food caused by drought, crops not producing, or government policies.) Abram told Sarai to say "no" to anyone who asked if they were married. He did not want to be killed by someone who wanted to take Sarai from him.

This flaw in Abram's character placed his wife in danger of being sexually assaulted by men who found her attractive, including the pharaoh. How did God respond to Abram's action? To protect Sarai, God caused a plague to spread throughout the pharaoh's house. When Abram confessed what he had done, Pharaoh told Abram and his crew to get out of his house immediately.

The second denial is found in Genesis 20. To paraphrase, Abram feared for his life so he told King Abimelek that Sarai was his sister and she validated his statement.

Scripture gives us this account in Genesis 20:13 where it tells that when God moved Abram from his father's household, Abram told Sarai that she could show her love for him by telling anyone who asked that he was her brother. According to Genesis 20:5, Abram and Sarai denied their marital status by promoting that she was his sister. So the king, thinking that she was available, took Sarai to make her his wife. Almighty God warned the king in a dream not to consummate the marriage by having sex with Sarai. He told the king to give Sarai back to her husband Abram who was a prophet. The king declared he was innocent of wrongdoing because Abram and Sarai claimed not to be married.

Genesis tells that King Abimelek accused Abram of placing the entire nation in danger by failing to admit that he and Sarai were husband and wife. Abram defended his actions claiming he had told the king this for self-protection and added that Sarai really was his sister, the daughter of his father, but not of his mother and then she became his wife (Genesis 20:12).

I am not focusing on if the marriage between Abram and Sarai was incestuous. Societal rules were different in those times. I am focusing on the fact that Abram twice denied his marital connection to Sarai. You can infer from the text that Abram placed his wife in harm's way twice. Abram's goal was to save his life instead of protecting his wife's life and wellbeing.

Husbands and boyfriends, think about similar life challenges where you thought you needed to protect yourself from a person, place, or thing and you covered yourself but exposed your wife or girlfriend to danger.

Similarly, some men have abandoned their wives and children or never accepted the fact that the baby was theirs. Families around the world are functioning out of God's ordained order where the female is the head of the household because the father has abdicated his God-given responsibility to be the head, regardless of what the cost is.

There are fathers who have earnestly tried to be part of their family's lives but some fathers are forced out of the home, incarcerated though they were falsely accused of crimes, or had a dependency on drugs or alcohol. The foster care system, grandparents, and relatives have been left to raise fatherless children. Fatherlessness increases the chance of systemic imprisonment, drug and alcohol addictions, and poverty, etc. It takes the grace of God to rescue fatherless children and make them a showpiece for the world to see and embrace.

Legacy, habit, and pattern of behavior _____

Abram denied his wife when he lied about his marital status. Later in this chapter you will see this negative pattern of behavior in his son Isaac and his grandson Jacob. Also, Jacob committed fraud and was a swindler. You are influenced by your parent's moral legacy, but I submit that you have the power to choose your response in every situation and to create your own positive pattern of behavior.

Are you ready to leave a positive legacy? A legacy is something that is handed down from one period of time to another period. This could mean money or property left to someone in a will for instance. Other words for legacy are bequest, inheritance, heritage (tradition or custom), endowment (donation), gift (contribution, present), patrimony, settlement (resolution, payment), birthright (inheritance).

A legacy can be negative or positive. For example, in this book, legacy references tradition and custom. Is a habit a legacy? Yes, habitual behavior is a legacy. A habit is a tendency, pattern, practice, inclination, custom, routine, or tradition.

For example, in the Jewish tradition, fathers were responsible to provide their sons with the knowledge, behavior, skills, and trades at the age of 12. In addition, fathers tend to find their sons a wife at the age of 20. In the African tradition, boys are preferred and once they are weaned by their mothers, they distance themselves from their mother in order to be trained by their fathers so that they can identify with masculine things.

In addition, a pattern of behavior can be passed down from one generation to another. What is a pattern of behavior? A pattern of behavior is something that you see over and over again that occurs in an individual, with couples, or in families. It can be passed on through observing certain behavior, language, or characteristics of a family member or by living in a particular community or environment.

32% of men say they attend religious services at least once a week while 40% of women say they attend religious services at least once a week. Yet it is the men who have the responsibility to be the Priest of their homes.

According to history, the influential religious leaders have been predominantly males. However, males attend religious services less often than their female counterparts. In the United States, for example, 60% of women say religion is "very important" in their lives, but only 47% of men respond this way according to a 2014 Pew Research Center Survey. American women also are more likely than American men to say they pray daily (64% vs. 47%). Some social scientists have argued that women are universally more religious than men across all societies, cultures, and faiths.

There are many reasons for these statistics. A few sociologists have theorized that the gender gap in religion is biological in nature, possibly stemming from higher levels of testosterone in men or other physical and genetic differences between the sexes. In my opinion, males tend to reject Christianity because they believe that it is a man-made religion. Males tend to reject parts or all of the Bible because they believe that the Bible was written by "the white man" or written by man to control the masses and/or to keep them enslaved by religion. A male member of my family shared his view that males/husbands tend to believe in God and attend church but not as much as their wives. They attend on Sunday and weekly Bible study but may not support other activities involving their church.

Many people think that white people in the West introduced Christianity. White people in the West did not introduce Christianity to Africans through slavery. To the contrary, it was Africa that helped to introduce Christianity as we now know it nearly 2,000 years prior. Though sometimes forgotten due to the Arab conquests of the continent, Africa boasts a long and rich Christian history, making the Christian religion just as much a traditional African religion as any other. That history began before the Bible was even completed according to Cole Brown, the founding pastor of Emmaus Church. I encourage you to pray about and research the history for yourself.

> **Note:** *The story found in Genesis 16–21 has been used to justify imperialism and a caste system among Arabs, Jews and African Americans to name a few. Imperialism is a policy of extending a country's power and influence through diplomacy or military imperialism. It occurs when a strong nation takes over a weaker nation or region and dominates its economic, political, and cultural life. A caste system is a type of social structure that divides people on the basis of inherited social status.*

God promises to bless Abraham's sons _____

In Genesis 14–15, God reiterates His covenant to Abram. Subsequently, Abram belts out that he has led and won many wars but does not yet have a family to lead. He asks God about the promise to bless him with a seed for his legacy. God reaffirms that yes, He will not only give Abram a seed but nations will come

69

from his seed. With that promise God changed their names to Abraham and Sarah.

Abraham and Sarah kept analyzing the calendar to determine the most fertile time to get pregnant to no avail. The fertility specialist informed Sarah that she was unable to have a child so Sarah commanded her handmaid (servant) Hagar to have the child for her as was custom at that time (Genesis 16). Remember that God had given Abraham and Sarah the promise of their own child though they both were old.

After the child was born, Sarah grew insecure, was enraged about her barrenness, and unhappy with too many females "in the kitchen." She was jealous that the child hadn't come out of her womb and that Abraham was showing too much attention to Hagar and his new-born son, Ishmael. Later, in keeping with God's word to Abraham and Sarah, Sarah conceived and had a son whom they named Isaac. When Sarah saw Ishmael teasing the baby Isaac, she grew angry. This uncontrolled emotion resulted in Sarah being mean-spirited and demeaning to Hagar. She convinced Abraham to put Hagar and her son out of their camp. Sarah was making life-changing decisions while she was in an irrational and erratic state of mind (Genesis 21).

God rescues and provides for Ishmael and his mother _____

Ishmael represents the Arabs and Isaac represents the Jewish people. For centuries, there have been conflicts in the Middle East over land and religion. Some people tend to feel that the Bible was manipulated to exclude Ishmael, the son of Hagar, from the covenant of promise. Ishmael means *God hears*. Further, Ishmael's name is a judgment against injustice within the family system whether it comes from domestic violence or family laws or stepchildren being mistreated (Genesis 1:20).

When Hagar and her son were about to starve, Hagar cried out to God for food, shelter, and clothing, God answered her prayers and opened her eyes to see the well that He provided. God promised to multiply Ishmael's seed because He heard Hagar cry about her unjust treatment (Genesis 21:13).

*Blended families: Sarah and Hagar, Ishmael and Isaac Sagas (Genesis 16:1-16 and Genesis 17:20 and 23)*_____

Ishmaelite and Arab people are ancestors of Ishmael. However, Ishmael was Abraham's first son and all those who are of the lineage of Ishmael who accept Jesus as Lord and Savior are of Abraham because of their faith in Jesus. More importantly, all of Abraham's heirs are included in the promises of the covenant. Genesis 12:2-3 states that Abraham's descendants will be blessed. This includes Ishmael. According to the Hebrew tradition recounted in Deuteronomy 21:15-17, the firstborn son gets double honor. This doesn't change because his mother was a maid.

In addition, in Genesis 21:18, God promised that kings would come out of Ishmael's lineage to be a great nation and Psalm 68:31 affirms that Ethiopians shall lift the hand to God and Princes shall rise up to rule Egypt. Psalm 68:1-6 speaks of God scattering His enemies and the enemies of the families of the earth. More importantly, God is providing homes for the fatherless and making provision for those who are widows.

Practical strategies to have an effective blended family _____

According to Shavonda Bean, Licensed Psychologist Associate, the American family structure is more diverse than ever. According to the Stepfather Foundation, a blended family results from divorce, separation, or death of a spouse. A blended family creates a shift from the original biologically bonded father, mother, and child. According to the United States Census Bureau, the average marriage in America lasts only 7 years. 75% of divorced people remarry and take on the role of a stepdad or stepmom. 50% of the 60 million stepchildren under the age of 13 are currently living with one biological parent and that parent's current partner according to the United States Bureau of Census.

Challenges for the children of blended families _____

According to research and observation, the living arrangements of children being shifted from one parent's house to the other can cause instability in the lives of children. Children tend to experience unsettling emotions due to the inconsistencies in home life. Often parents play "good cop, bad cop" to get their child to side with them. Giving children too much information too soon thrusts children into an adult world that they are not ready for. Parents attempt to get the children to play referee and tend to force the children to choose the one they want to live with.

The negative residual effects of an unstable blended family _____

Innocent children tend to feel confused, ashamed, fearful, insecure, anxious, and abandoned. They often blame themselves for the divorce and usually their grades decline. Also, many times they experience emotional outbursts, promiscuity, and alcohol abuse as a result of this instability.

Create a healthy and loving environment for children to thrive in life and academically _____

On the other hand, when stepfathers and stepmothers use the following good strategies, they increase the chances of having an effective blended family. You have been given an awesome responsibility to shape and influence your stepchild in their childhood and adult life.

Be intentional when parenting; do not wing it! Create a united front to grow and develop your child _____

Children tend to manipulate their stepparents and cause them to fight with each other. You must come to a mutually respectful agreement on discipline, curfew, finances, play dates, child rearing, and other family "rules," otherwise your child will create havoc in your home. Have family meetings and assure the child that he or she is an important part of the family. Explain your role and responsibility to them and the important role they play in the family. Be sure to pace yourself with creating your new home. Use authentic teachable moments to give your child small portions of information. It is important to give them a voice and a safe place to vent when needed.

Visitation

Develop an agreeable visitation schedule and include routines. Be consistent and be courteous when you cannot keep your visitation. If you cannot come up with a workable plan, it increases the likelihood that a judge at Family Court or a Child Custody/Visitation Attorney will set a plan and put your child first.

Favoritism

Love all your children but demonstrate your love according to how your child is wired. Some children do not respond to hugs and kisses while others do. Read *The Five Love Languages of Children* by Gary Chapman and D. Ross Campbell. Provide for all your children: do not give unfair preferential treatment to one child at the expense of the other. You will read later in this chapter how Jacob favored Joseph and that was a catalyst to sibling rivalry. For more resources, contact The National Stepfamily Resource Center at 1-303-555-1234.

Your responsibility is to create a safe, secure, and stimulating home for your child _____

Try not to argue in front of the children. It is healthy for your child to see you have heated debates where you agree to disagree and remain amiable toward one another. Remember to present that united front. Definitely do not physically or emotionally abuse one another. If your relationship turns abusive, speak with your spouse to let them know that you will not tolerate abuse and neglect. If talking to them doesn't work, speak to a trusted family member or friend. If it escalates, call the National Domestic Violence Hotline at 1-800-799-7233. Also, to strengthen your marriage, contact the National Organization for Marriages at 1-888-894-3604.

Comparison of Abraham and God
Abraham and Sarah were given a son whom they named Isaac. Genesis 22:2 tells that God instructed Abraham to "take your son Isaac, whom you love" and make him a burnt offering. This is the first mention of the word love or beloved in the Bible. Abraham followed God's command with sorrow, but Isaac's life was spared at the last minute when God provided a ram for Abraham to sacrifice instead.

God offered up His only Son to the world (John 3:15-16) just as Abraham offered up Isaac to God. Jesus was God's beloved son (Matthew 3:17) and Isaac was Abraham's beloved son (Genesis 12:2). Unconditional love is what God and Abraham had for their sons. Deuteronomy 5:10, 7:7, 7:13 affirms that God lavished His unfailing love to thousands of generations. The Greek word for this love is *agape*. This is the ultimate form of love that God demonstrated for humankind.

Lessons to glean

- **A father's instruction** — During the famine in Canaan, Isaac was contemplating his upward mobility, so he travelled to Gerar. The LORD told Isaac, "Do not relocate to Egypt but wait for me to tell you where to relocate. I will be with you and I will bless you and your offspring."

- **A son's obedience** — Isaac listened to God.

- **Isaac is overcome with the same temptation as his father, Abraham** — While in Gerar, handsome men asked about Isaac's wife, wanting to know if she "was taken." Isaac replied, "No, she is my sister." OOPS! Isaac lied! Abraham's son Isaac lied in the same way his father did. Does this suggest "like father, like son"? No, Isaac made a conscious decision to lie. This was an opportunity for Isaac to learn from his father's sin and do the opposite of his father.

- **Sin exposed** — Lo and behold, Abimelech, King of the Philistines, just happened to look out his window one beautiful day and saw Isaac kissing, fondling, and hugging Rebecca. Here comes the drama! King Abimelech challenges Isaac, "Man, you told me that she was your sister."

- **God's protection through an ungodly source**
  — Although the king was furious, he decreed
  that anyone who tried to have sexual relations
  with Isaac's wife would be put to death. God
  caused all the good, bad, and the ugly to work
  out for the good of Isaac and his offspring. Genesis 26:12-14 reports that Isaac had a 100-fold
  harvest and greatly increased his flocks, herds,
  and servants. King Abimelech saw that Isaac
  was growing mightier than the king himself
  and that Isaac's God was powerful because
  Isaac always seemed to prosper. He was afraid
  of Isaac and made him leave his kingdom.

  Although Isaac lied in the same manner that his
  father had lied because he was afraid for his life,
  Isaac still loved God and built an altar to God
  (Genesis 26:25).

Jacob (trickster and swindler)

It is important to know that God's chosen people
experienced tragedies and challenges in their lives. The
blessing is that God revealed Himself to them in the
midst of their challenges. This is Jacob's story.

Jacob stole his older brother Esau's birthright when
he tricked their father Isaac. Jacob then ran away to
his uncle in fear of his life. Jacob fell in love with his
cousin Rachel but was tricked by his uncle into marrying Rachel's older sister, Leah. The trickster got tricked
himself. Jacob eventually got to marry Rachel so he had
two wives, Leah and Rachel, and he married their hand-
maidens as well. Although Leah produced sons, Rachel

was barren until God gave her Joseph. Later, Rachel gave birth to Benjamin, but she died in childbirth.

Jacob given a new name by God
In Genesis 32:27-28 God asked Jacob his name and Jacob replied, "Jacob." God responded that his name would no longer be Jacob but now his name would be Israel. His descendants became known as Israelites. In verse 29, Jacob named the location Peniel (meaning face of God) because this is where he saw God face-to-face, and his life was preserved.

Jacob experienced both miracles and tragedy. Joseph was his favored son and Jacob treated him differently than his brothers. In this story, we will see how God caused the tragedies of Joseph to work in His favor. God worked bad things for good once again in Joseph's story.

Joseph _____

When a dream looks like a nightmare and promises look like disappointment, don't downsize your dream.
Joseph is the son of Jacob, the grandson of Isaac, and great-grandson of Abraham. The Bible provides us with a snapshot of the life, struggles, situations, weaknesses, strengths, and temperament of Joseph.

Favoritism brings dissension among siblings
Joseph's relationship with people helped to shape his journey in life. His father, Jacob, showed partiality in parenting and spoiled Joseph so in his early life Joseph treated his brothers unfairly.

Joseph knew his father loved him more than his brothers. Jacob favored Joseph because he was the son of Rachel whom Jacob loved and because Joseph was a son of his old age. This caused Jacob to display his love differently with Joseph than his other sons. He gave Joseph an expensive and colorful coat. In contrast, Jacob bought his other sons plainer tunics to wear.

What was so special about Joseph's coat of many colors? This coat represented a position of special favoritism and honor with his father. In light of the fact that Joseph was next to the youngest son and the favored son, his brothers hated him (Genesis 37:4). Joseph did not help matters with his behavior toward them. At the age of 17, Joseph was feeding the flock with his stepbrothers from Bilhah and Zilpah, his father's wives who were also servants of Leah and Rachel. Joseph was a tattletale. He ran to his father and gave him evil reports about his brothers' conduct (Genesis 39:1-2).

The ability to dream _____

The Bible tells about Joseph having special dreams that he described to his brothers. In order to understand the importance of Joseph's dreams, it is helpful to understand the historical context in which Joseph was born and the purpose of his birth.

Genesis 37:7-8 tells of two dreams Joseph had where his father and brothers bowed down to him. When Joseph told his brothers and his father about these dreams, the brothers became angry with him and threw him in a pit. Then they decided to sell him to the Egyptians. Joseph was able to do well in Egypt and received a promotion in the Pharaoh's service. Then lies were told about him, and he was thrown in prison and forgotten about. After he interpreted some dreams for fellow prisoners, he was called upon to interpret a dream for the Pharaoh. When he interpreted the dream, the Pharaoh promoted him to Governor of Egypt.

The Power of Forgiveness

When his brothers came to Egypt to get food for their families because of a great famine, they came before Joseph, but they did not recognize him although Joseph recognized them. Here is the lesson in this story. Joseph was in a position of power and could help or harm his brothers who had sold him into slavery. He had the opportunity to hold a grudge or to forgive them. He forgave them in order to truly experience peace in his new station in life.

After Joseph told his brothers to go and get Jacob, Joseph saw the dream coming to pass. In the meantime, Joseph's brothers packed up their stuff and traveled back to Canaan to tell their father, Jacob, the good but unbelievable news. Reuben, the eldest son, might have said something like, "Look, Father, we have to talk to you about an urgent matter; I think you had better sit down for this one. Your son Joseph is alive, and he has become the Governor of Egypt and you must quickly pack and relocate to Egypt" (Genesis 45:24-28).

Jacob did not believe his sons at first and was disturbed by the news. When a person has a pattern of lying, this pattern of behavior increases people's doubt about anything the person says. To this end, God stepped in to convince Jacob that this was a God ordained move (Genesis 46:1-27). How did God reveal to Jacob that his sons were telling the truth? To paraphrase Genesis 46:2-3, God spoke to Israel in the visions of the night, "Here am I. I am the God, the God of your father: do not fear to go down to Egypt, I declare that in Egypt I will make you a great nation."

After Jacob received this "night vision," he got up to prepare for his relocation from Beersheba to Egypt. Sixty-six family members came out of Jacob's loins plus Joseph and his two sons who were already in Egypt; therefore, the total number in Jacob's family was 70.

The nations were counting on him _____

Joseph saved his entire family. He told his brothers that although they intended to do evil to him, God sent him to Egypt ahead of them to save them (Genesis 50). "The LORD was with Joseph, and he was a prosperous man; and he was in the house of his master the Egyptian" (Genesis 39:2). Think about how one man made a huge difference for his family. Ask yourself, "What difference can I make in my family?"

God's promise to the 12 tribes _____

The book of Exodus begins with the genealogy of the children of Israel, the Israelites who traveled to Egypt). "These are the names of the children of Israel which came into Egypt: Reuben, Issachar, Naphtali, Simeon, Zebulun, Gad, Levi, Benjamin, Asher, Judah and Dan. Every household travelled with Jacob, 70 souls came out of Jacob" (Exodus 1:5). Remember, Joseph was already in Egypt and had two sons there. His father and brothers came years after he had arrived in Egypt. God's promise was that they would always be His people and He would be always their God.

God's promises were first made to Abram in Genesis 12:1-3 and carried down to his descendants. We explored the writings on the confirmations and affirmations of these promises, which are in Genesis 15, 17, and 22 in the previous chapter of this book. How is this life lesson through the patriarchs significant to you? When God makes a promise to you, Satan, the devil, will attempt to assassinate you, your character, and your life spiritually, emotionally, socially, relationally, mentally, intellectually, and financially. Satan seeks to work through your friends, family, and strangers. However, the good news is God will use every device of the enemy to bring out all that is good in you. *God will see to it that you receive all His benefits and experience His unending love.*

God fulfills His promise by multiplying husbands, wives, and children _____

The Israelites lived in Egypt for centuries and eventually became an enslaved people there. Our abundant God saw to it that the children of Israel grew to 600,000 men. Note, this number didn't include women and children (Exodus 12:37). This number was recorded while the Israelites were still in slavery.

Why is this important today? Because Elohim, another name for our All Powerful and All Creative God, will create, preserve, recreate, and sustain you and your family in the middle of slavery, killing, stealing, destruction, ethnic cleansing, genocide, infanticide, homicide, suicide, and inflicting harm to ourselves. God's will and desire is to heal, deliver, rescue, develop, and grow your family as well as bring your family out of bondages and sinful patterns of behavior. He wants to give your family a fresh start and demonstrate His unending love and mercy to generations to come. Please give Him an opportunity to show Himself marvelous on your family's behalf. God delights in increasing and preserving all the families of the earth. Let's read further to see how He rescued the children of Israel.

Fear and hatred were the reasons for the children of Israel's enslavement

God allowed their enemies to dominate the Israelites for a time, but He never left them. No, their enemies saw that God's promises were coming to pass. The children of Israel were producing many offspring as God promised. God is a God who is revealed as the God of more than enough, therefore, He carried out His promise to increase and preserve the children of Israel. The Egyptians were fearful of their numbers and kept the Israelites enslaved.

The book of Genesis ends with the death of Joseph (Genesis 50:22-26) _____

Although Joseph lived in Egypt, he knew that Egypt was not his home and that one day he would live in another homeland. Before Joseph's death, he told his brothers "when I die, take my bones to Canaan, the land of promise." Joseph realized that even in his death, he would experience the "life" of the promise that God covenanted to his great grandfather, Abraham, his grandfather, Isaac, and to his father, Jacob. The book of Hebrews 11:22 records that Joseph lived by faith when he gave this commandment to his relatives. Although Joseph was 110 years old and on his death bed, he did not give up hope that he would experience the Promised Land but allowed his faith and dependency on God to propel him forward to an eternal city.

The life of the resilient Joseph, son of Jacob, is a typology of the life of Christ. Joseph eventually saved his family from famine and helped them start a new life in Egypt. Jesus was graciously sent to the world from Heaven. Herod wish to do Him harm because he thought Jesus was going to be a rival for his kingdom so an angel of the Lord came to Joseph, Mary's soon-to-be husband, and warned him to go to Egypt to be safe. When Jesus returned to His people, He showed them the way to new life and through Jesus those who believe are saved. This will be covered in more detail in chapter 7.

Chapter 3 — Questions to extend learning

Why did God tell Abram to leave his family and country?

_____

_____

_____

_____

_____

_____

List ways you plan to leave a positive legacy for your family.

_____

_____

_____

_____

_____

_____

CHAPTER 4

Moses — a foster child who became a great leader

THE MOSAIC COVENANT — MOSES'S LIFE CLASSROOM

- The children of Israel are tested at Sinai.
- The 5th Covenant — Mosaic (Genesis 19:5) — conditional covenant
- The 5th Dispensation — Law (Exodus 19:1)

Consider being a foster or respite parent; you may be grooming a revolutionary leader!

The book of Exodus details Moses's father and mother were from the tribe of Levi. Moses's ethnic background was Hebrew, but he was raised in the house of the Egyptian pharaoh by the pharaoh's daughter. She was single but she provided food, shelter, clothing, love, and a nanny to babysit Moses, which signifies that she was rich. Guess what? Moses's child care provider was his own mother; however, that was a secret while he was raised in the court of the Egyptian pharaoh (Exodus 2:5-10). So Moses was raised by foster parents!

The Congressional Coalition on Adoption reports that in the United States 397,122 children are living without permanent families in the foster care system. According to Child Information—United Nations International Children's Emergency Fund (UNICEF, 2011)—there are an estimated 153 million orphans around the world who have lost one parent. Further, there are 17,900,000 orphans who have lost both parents.

For information about adoption, call 703-299-6633; or about fostering, call 800-557-5238.

God, Moses, and the unburnable bush

Moses committed a crime and had to flee to the desert. He met and married Zipporah. While Moses was pasturing and tending the flock of Jethro, his father-in-law, he led the flock to the far side of the desert and came to Horeb, the mountain of God (Exodus 3:1-4). It was on this mountain that the angel of the LORD appeared to Moses. The angel of the LORD is God. So let's continue to see how God revealed Himself to Moses. The angel of the LORD appeared to Moses in a blazing flame from within a bush. What got Moses's attention was that the bush was on fire, but the bush did not burn. So Moses decided to go see why the bush did not burn up. When the LORD saw that he had come to look, God called to him from in the bush, "Moses, Moses!" And Moses answered, "Here am I." The LORD said, "Do not come any further, take off your sandals from your feet, for the place on which you are standing is holy ground" (Exodus 3:5).

Our lesson

When your heavenly, living, and almighty Father God calls you, no matter what state or condition you are in, you must answer just as Moses did: "Here am I."

God doesn't want us to hold back our will, emotion, mindset, lifestyle, body, or soul. He desires for us to willingly yield to Him and come to Him to cleanse and free us from all our bondages. We have to yield ourselves to the LORD before, during, and after a mountain top experience in order to maintain that penthouse experience. Otherwise we may fall off the mountain top. The LORD got Moses's attention in the backside of the desert by a blazing fire in the middle of the bush, but God did not allow the element to burn or to disintegrate the bush. Wow! The Bible gives us hope that in the midst of fiery trials we will not be burned.

Holiness is one of the many attributes of God

Why did God tell Moses to take off his sandals and come no further? Because God revealed His holiness to Moses. Moses hid his face because he was afraid to look at God. Moses's first encounter with God is that Moses hides his face from God. This reflects that Moses acknowledges his humanity and challenges (Exodus 3:5-6). He probably did not feel righteous and did not want to gaze upon God and die as a result (Exodus 19:20).

Jehovah God sees and cares about your pain and sufferings

Our heavenly and merciful Father is an all-seeing God and He is a Jehovah Jireh who always provides humanity with a man/woman to accomplish His perfect and divine will in the earth. To paraphrase

Exodus 3:7-10, The LORD said, "I have indeed seen the misery of my people in Egypt. I have heard them crying out because of their slave drivers, and I am concerned about their suffering. So I have come down to rescue them from the hand of the Egyptians and to bring them up out of that land into a good and spacious land, a land flowing with milk and honey. The land will be inhabited by the Canaanites, Hittites, Amorites, Perizzites, Hivites, and the Jebusites, but with my help you will drive them out gradually. Moses, we have work to do because the cry of the Israelites has reached me, and I have seen the way the Egyptians are oppressing them. So now, go. I am sending you to Pharaoh to bring my people, the Israelites, out of Egypt."

In Exodus 3:8 God said to Moses that He had "come down" to deliver them. That does not mean God literally came down to earth to rescue the children of Israel out of bondage. No, God did not literally come down to earth to talk to Pharaoh to urge him to let His people go; God sent and empowered Moses, his representative, to be the messenger.

Moses feels he is inadequate but God reassurance Moses of His constant presence. "Who am I that you want to work through me?" (Exodus 3:11)

In Exodus 3:10 God tells Moses He is sending him to Pharaoh. Moses responds, "Who am I that I should go to Pharaoh and bring the children of Israel out of Egypt?"

Let's focus on "who am I?" Moses is asking this question from a feeling of inadequacy about what God wanted him to do. Every human being will ask this monumental question at some point. The broader question is *"Why am I here?"* Or, put another way, *"What is the reason for my existence?"*

It is important for everyone to know who they are and what their God-given purpose in life is. Moses learned "who he was" by learning "who God is." Similarly, you can learn who you are by learning who God is. God is your Father, thus, your creator. Only your Heavenly Father knows why He created you. No one in the entire world can answer that old question but Almighty God. With this in mind, you must connect and commune with your Supreme Being in order to understand yourself as a "human being."

Let's take this journey to see how God continued to introduce Himself and His presence to Moses, thus answering Moses's "Who am I?" question. I believe that Moses represents our life in that He is God's vehicle to convey to the world that God wants to have a tangible relationship with His children and that we can experience all that life has in store for us with a compassionate God by our side. In essence, God wants us to have His constant presence and power within us, with us, and upon us.

Our Father's token
(Our Father will never abandon us)

During the process of God introducing Himself to

Moses, Moses argued with God about his inadequacies. God reassured Moses about His continued presence. Thus, God reaffirmed His presence with us (Exodus 3:12) saying, "Certainly I will be with you; and this shall be a token unto thee, that I have sent thee: When thou hast brought forth the people out of Egypt, ye shall serve God upon the mountain."

God's name depicts His character and abilities

In Exodus 3:14-15, Moses anxiously said to God, "I am going to follow your instructions and tell them the God of our fathers has sent me to you, Lord, but I know the children of Israel; they are going to ask me, what is His name? What should I say to them?" In verse 14 God said to Moses, "I AM THAT I AM: and then He said, Thus shalt thou say unto the children of Israel, I AM hath sent me unto you." To paraphrase verse 15 God instructs Moses to tell the children of Israel the LORD, God of your fathers, the God of Abraham, the God of Isaac and the God of Jacob, has sent me to you. This is my name forever, and this is my memorial unto all generations. Moses was instructed to represent God, he was to tell them about the everlasting name of God: I AM THAT I AM.

*Practical application of our
Heavenly Father's name* _____

Some people randomly study the names of God without the realization that God is revealing Himself to us in the context of the following:

- Who He is apart from His children

- Who He is in relation to His children

- How He is to be introduced to the nations of the world

In Exodus 6:3 and Genesis 17:1, God made Himself known to Abraham, Isaac, and Jacob by the name of "Almighty God" (El Shaddai in Hebrew) which means that He was all powerful. In the book of Exodus, He chooses to reveal Himself differently. Moses had a dangerous mission, goal, and vision to carry out for God. However, before he was to carry out this seemingly impossible mission, God needed to make sure that Moses realized the blessing and strength of His eternal presence. So at the onset of Moses's ministry, God introduces Himself as Yahweh, a God who is present. To this end, God's special covenant name as revealed in the Bible is **Yahweh** translated as "**LORD**." Genesis 2:4 reads. "In the day that the *LORD* God made the earth and the heavens…" and Exodus 3:14 reads, "I AM THAT I AM." Here Yahweh is God present and active in the life of Moses. *Yahweh is the LORD'S presence and spirit with His people.*

The Mosiac covenant corresponds with the fundamental promises of the Abrahamic covenant — God's desire "to be a God unto thee" as written in Genesis 17:7. Moses is a type of Christ as he is to save God's people just as Jesus who is called Emmanuel, which means God with us, is sent to save God's people under the new covenant (Matthew 1:23). Jesus also calls himself by the name "I am" frequently in the Gospel of John. For example, John 8:58 reads: "Very truly I tell you," Jesus answered, "before Abraham was born, I am!"

We see God as Yahweh with Moses in that He begins to demonstrate to Moses, the elders, and the children of Israel His mighty hand. Today, all the families of the earth can experience the living presence of God Himself every day.

Moses as intercessor who entered into sessions with God on the behalf of the children of Israel

In Exodus 3:18 God tells Moses what to expect when he goes to the Israelites and Pharaoh: "And they shall hearken to thy voice: and thou shalt come, thou and the elders of Israel, unto the king of Egypt, and you shall say unto him, The LORD God of the Hebrews hath met with us: and now let us go, we beseech thee, three day's journey into the wilderness, that we may sacrifice to the LORD our God."

Moses went to Pharaoh and told him to let his people go. Moses calls the children of Israel his people as an intercessor on behalf of God for the Israelites. Were they Moses's people? No, they were emphatically God's people. Moses is a type of Christ acting for God to save God's people; therefore, as Christ calls us His children, Moses called the children of Israel his children.

In other words, Moses was acting on behalf of God. The words "my people" depict ownership and a personal relationship between Moses and the children of Israel and God. In the dispensation of grace, we do not need types, shadows, and school masters because Christ has appeared as our savior, mediator, intercessor, father, and elder brother. No one but God has ownership of another human being. With this in mind, spiritual leaders, you are a representative of God, you are to "re-present" God to the people. You are a carrier of the Spirit of God. You are a watchmen and overseer for their souls.

After a series of horrific plagues, Pharaoh let God's people go. Then he took a second thought and changed his mind. Pharaoh sent his army to bring back Moses and the Israelites. The Israelites were at the Red Sea. God told Moses to stretch out his hand over the sea and God caused a path to open up by holding the waters back by a strong east wind all that night. God made a path where the waters were divided so the children of Israel could make it safely across the sea, but God told Moses to stretch out his hand again over the sea and God caused the waters to fall and all the Egyptian pursuers were drowned.

Personally guard your freedom to worship God _____

Satan's bondage and oppression of people is to keep humanity from acknowledging, believing, and accepting Jesus as Lord and Savior and living out their specific purpose in life. In the book of Exodus, the issue Satan had with the children of Israel, God's people, was *their worship of the true and living God*. Satan comes to *kill the relationship* with Jesus Christ so that men, women, boys, and girls cannot worship their creator in a healthy and trusting way. Satan raised up Pharaoh to enslave the people of God and to prevent them from serving God. However God always has a plan to bring His people back to Him so that He can be a nurturing Father to them. Exodus 19:4 reminds us: "Ye have seen what I did unto the Egyptians, and how I bare you on eagles' wings, and brought you unto myself."

The LORD had an assignment for Moses to fulfill, thus Moses was called upon to obey and respond to God's call. Upon Moses's visit with God, Moses's face began to change. In God's presence, people, places, and things change. For example, your mind, will, and volition conform to the mind and will of God when you walk with Him. Moses reflected God because he was a representative of God.

Let's look at the prefix and suffix of representative. The prefix in representative is "re" which mean to do again and the suffix "present" is to be present or to be there. In other words, Moses was to re-present God or to be present as God would be present as a spokesperson, ambassador, or delegate of God. In order for Moses to be able to effectively represent God and lead God's people, he had to acknowledge and receive God's instruction. His father-in-law, Jethro, gave him wise advice once the people were in the desert. Let's see how Moses learns to be God-focused and not people-focused. Exodus 18:13-27 shows us the wise counsel of God concerning Moses. God told Jethro to tell Moses to bring people's causes to God. In addition, he admonished Moses to teach, explain, and model the ordinances and laws in order for the people to learn to walk in the way of God.

As Christians, we must learn obedience in order to grow and experience the development milestones just as a newborn baby growing through adulthood does. Similarly, as an ambassador and representative of God, my role is to introduce God to the world. I am to tell of the mega God in the earth and His deep passion to enter into a vibrant relationship with all. I believe that the families of the earth can have a passion and desire to want to meet with God and spend time in His presence as the children of Israel desired. The New Testament Church can help create this passion as it:

- listens to the voice of God.

- gathers its leaders.

- sends its leaders to political representatives.

- develops its leaders to speak on behalf of God and His church.

- understands the dispensations, times, and seasons of our Christian journey.

- underscores the importance of the relationship of leaders with the LORD and the guidance He gives.

- develops leaders to possess the ability to declare and decree freedom on behalf of those who are poor, blind, in prison, and enslaved.

- trains leaders to spur a desire among the congregants so that they are eager to sacrifice themselves to the LORD.

The Ten Commandments compared to the Two Commandments

Moses led the Israelites into the desert where they remained for 40 years and experienced many of God's miracles. During this time in the desert, God called Moses to the mountaintop and delivered the Ten Commandments to him. The institution of the law and the Ten Commandments in Exodus reveal the importance of choice and responsibility in God's Kingdom. God blesses obedience and punishes disobedience.

The Ten Commandments record man's obligations to God and to man (humanity) _____

These are the obligations to God — Exodus 20:3–4, 7–8

- "Thou shalt have no other gods before me" (Exodus 20:3).

- "Thou shalt not have any graven image" (Exodus 20:4).

- "Thou shalt not take the name of the LORD thy God in vain" (Exodus 20:7).

- "Remember the Sabbath day" (Exodus 20:8).

These are the obligations to Man (Humanity) — Exodus 20:12–17

- Honor thy father and mother (Exodus 20:12).

- Thou shalt not kill (Exodus 20:13).

- Thou shalt not commit adultery (Exodus 20:14).

- Thou shalt not steal (Exodus 20:15).

- Thou shalt not bear false witness (Exodus 20:16).

- Thou shalt not covet (Exodus 20:17).

In order to develop a character of love and kindness, you must obey the commands of God.

In order for mankind to be kind to one another, they must first be kind and respond "in kind" to God. Thus, the first four of the Ten Commandments relate to man's relationship to God as our creator and deliverer. The latter six relate to Man's relationship to one another.

Jesus came to fulfill the types and shadows of the Ten Commandments. He is the God of Glory and the Lord of Love. Jesus gave us the Great Commandment: "Love the Lord your God with all your heart and with all your soul and with all your mind. This is the first and greatest commandment. And the second is like it: Love your neighbor as yourself. All the Law and the Prophets hang on these two commandments" (Matthew 22:37-40) (cf. Leviticus 19:18).

John 3:16 tells us that God loves the world so much that He sent His son to save us. As a former sinner, I learned Christ and forgiveness through my Father's love. I have a good memory. Having a great memory is good when it comes to things that I need to remember.

To the contrary, it is a challenge when I need to forgive and show love. God is good because I have learned to focus on God's love for me, and now I practice extending love to others.

Why are the interactions and relationships important to Christians today? _____

1 Corinthians 13:13 says: "and now abideth faith, hope, charity, these three, but the greatest of these is charity." Love (charity) ranks above ministry, faith, or the possession of spiritual gifts. In essence, God is love, and God has given us a spirit of love, power, and a sound mind. God commands us to love Him with all of our heart, and with all our soul, and with our entire mind (Matthew 22:37-40). Then He tells us to love one another. This passage suggests that when we recognize and accept the love of God, we can reflect His love and we can mirror His love to love and accept ourselves and love others with the love of the LORD. In order to identify with Him, He empowers us to love Him and one another. It is out of our love for God that we can love ourselves. Further, God gives the higher degree of importance to His character (love), which is His Christ-like character. We must yield to Christ to become more and more like Him and promote Christ-like characteristics.

The Bible clearly states in John 1:17 that the law was given by Moses, but grace and truth came by Jesus Christ. Anytime God wants to reveal Himself, He usually works through mankind. To Moses and the Israelites, God gave the law. Through Christ, God granted mankind grace and truth through the sacrifice of His Son. Exhibiting God's love and embracing Christ-like characteristics help us carry out God's work under His new covenant.

God's compassion

What happened to the children of Israel is a far cry from what God had promised Abraham. Israel was taken into slavery for 400 years. Regardless of Israel's captivity, their God performed miracles to fulfill His promise to His children.

*Summary*_____

The Israelites lived in slavery to Pharaoh. The people cried out to the God of their forefathers. God heard them and remembered His covenant with Abraham, with Isaac, and with Jacob and sent Moses as his representative to bring them out of slavery. Through Moses, God called the people of Israel to get up and leave their position of slavery in Egypt. After a series of ten plagues upon the land of Egypt, God brought the Israelites "out of Egypt with great power and with a mighty hand" (Exodus 34:5). As God delivered the Israelites, they moved into the desert by way of the Red Sea and eventually came to Mount Sinai in the Sinai Peninsula.

Exodus records more miracles of God than any other book in the Old Testament. God rescued and delivered His people as He guided them into the unfamiliar desert. There, God instituted His system of laws, gave instruction in worship, and established His people as the nation of Israel. Exodus is a book of tremendous spiritual significance.

Life Lessons

Slavery was real. Israel's slavery is a picture of man's slavery to sin. Ultimately only through God's divine guidance and leadership can we escape our slavery to sin. However, God also directed the people through the godly leadership of Moses. Typically, God leads us into freedom today through wise leadership and through His word.

Have you wondered if your family will survive killings, stolen years, and self or imposed destruction? Do you think that your family is cursed because of all the tragedies and challenges? Do people look at you and say, "Wow, I do not know anyone who has gone through as many horrible and tragic events as your family has."

If you answered yes to any of those questions, you are not alone. The children of Israel had been crying out to God for deliverance. God was concerned about their suffering, and He rescued them. He will rescue you and your family. The children of Israel were saved from the hand of the Egyptians; however, the Egyptians perished in the sea (Exodus14:21-31).

Chapter 4 — Questions to extend learning

Describe how you manage anger and list two ways that you use to maintain your cool in a heated situation.

_____

_____

_____

_____

_____

_____

Circle the ways that you would be willing help a child in foster care and/or the foster care system.

- Become a foster parent

- Adopt a child

- Donate to the cause

- Become a mentor

- Volunteer

CHAPTER 5

Davidic Covenant — David's Life Classroom

- **When your father doesn't acknowledge your existence, Your Heavenly Father will make you king.**

- **The 6th Covenant — Davidic (2 Samuel 7:16, Psalms 89) — unconditional covenant**

- **The 5th Dispensation — Law continues (Exodus 19:1)**

- **A story of adultery, conspiracy to murder, abuse of political power, and God's forgiveness**

Let's start with the words of Apostle Peter in Acts 2:29-30. "Men and brethren, let me freely speak unto you of the patriarch David that he is both dead and buried, and his sepulcher is with us unto this day. Therefore being a prophet, and knowing that God had sworn with an oath to him, that of the fruit of his loins, according to the flesh, He would raise up Christ to sit on his throne." King David's throne is a channel to the eternal throne of God. This scripture also supports the fact that Christ would be raised up from the dead and exalted to sit on his throne. Let's see how David entered into a covenantal relationship with God prior to his coronation as Israel's second king.

In times past, Israel did not have a government with

kings; God was their king, and they were governed and lived under His rule. However, Israel was not satisfied with this type of theocratic government, so they asked God for a king. It was not God's perfect and divine will, but He granted them their request. To this end, the people were excited that Saul was to be king. He received his "coronation" and was anointed by Samuel to be king over Israel (1 Samuel 15:1). In 1 Samuel 15:2, the LORD told King Saul to destroy Amalek totally, including men, women, infants, cattle, sheep, camels, and donkeys. In 1 Samuel 15:8, we see Saul disobeyed the LORD by sparing the life of Agag, the King of the Amalekites. Verse 9 then describes how Saul kept back the best of the sheep, cattle, fatlings, and lambs and everything deemed as good. He had everything that was vile and refuse destroyed. God expressed His emotions with man as He did during the days of Noah. In 1 Samuel 15:11 God says, "It repenteth me that I have set up Saul to be king: for he is turned back from following me, and hath not performed my commandments." It goes on to say Samuel grieved and cried unto the LORD all night.

Note, the LORD equates disobedience as turning back from Him. This is important because we do not want to turn back from following our Heavenly Father, but we want to listen to His voice and please Him.

Be obedient to God's way

King Saul thought that he obeyed the LORD because he sacrificed the best of the sheep and cattle to the LORD and destroyed the rest. Some may say this is partial obedience, but to God Saul's actions were total disobedience and his disobedience cost Saul his throne. Verse 23 goes on to read: "For rebellion is as the sin of witchcraft, and stubbornness is as iniquity and idolatry. Because thou hast rejected the word of the Lord, He hath also rejected thee from being King."

In the master plan of God

- Do you believe that preparation precedes opportunity?

- Have you ever been overlooked?

- Are you more than your physical body?

- Who is misjudging you because of your looks or personal traits?

God as Elohim is all powerful; He has predetermined the end before the beginning. Despite the disobedience of King Saul, God's plan and purposes of Jesus coming through the lineage of David did not change. 1 Samuel 16:1 reads: "... the LORD said unto Samuel, How long wilt thou mourn for Saul, seeing I have rejected him from reigning over Israel? Fill thine horn with oil, and go, I will send thee to Jesse the Bethelhemite: for I have provided me a king among his sons."

God loves you and looks at your heart _____

It is your spirit that gets God's attention, not your outward appearance. More importantly, the word declares:

"Every way of man is right in his own eyes: but the LORD pondereth the hearts" (Proverbs 21:2). 1 Samuel 16:7 says: "But the LORD said to Samuel, look not on his countenance or the height of his stature; because I have refused him: for the LORD seeth not as man seeth: for man looketh on the outward appearance, but the LORD looketh on the heart." God is not intimidated by body piercing, body tattoos, ghetto fabulous, or geekdified. Whether you live in a whorehouse, poor house, or penthouse, God still cares about you.

Get the youngest! _____

So David's saga begins. Jesse had eight sons. He called his strong sons forward for Samuel to see who would be the next king. The oldest, Abinadab, first and the next oldest, Shammah, on down through seven sons were presented to Samuel. To paraphrase 1 Samuel 16:11, Samuel turned to Jesse and asked if he had another son. Jesse replied that his youngest son was out keeping the sheep. Samuel instructed Jesse to call David to come to him. In 1 Samuel 16:12, the LORD said: "Arise, anoint him: for this is he." Verse 13a continues: "Then Samuel took the horn of oil, and anointed him in the midst of his brethren; and the spirit of the LORD came upon David from that day forward."

We can infer from this chapter that David's own father did not acknowledge him as his son. Also, Jesse ignored David because he was the youngest and was a shepherd boy. You may be able to identify or be able to make a connection with David if you have ever been ignored or passed over by your father or those around you.

God's covenant with David _____

2 Samuel 7:16 describes how God made a covenant with David: "And thine house and thy kingdom shall be established forever before thee: thy throne shall be established forever."

In essence, David's house, kingdom, and throne will be established forever. Included in verses 12-16 we read: "And when the days be fulfilled *I will* establish my kingdom, he shall build a house for my name, *I will* be his father and he shall be my son." Note, in Genesis 3:15a, God initiated, the "I will" statement when He was speaking to the serpent: "I will put an enmity between thee and the woman." Psalm 89:3-4 affirms this covenant: God says, "I have made a covenant with my chosen, I have sworn unto David my servant. Thy seed will I establish forever, and build up thy throne to all generations. Selah!" (Selah means to stop and think. Also, it can be a long pause in music.)

God did not fail to keep His covenant with David, this covenant was conditional because when the Davidic kings and the children of Israel disobeyed God and persisted in apostasy, God removed the kings or allowed their enemies to take them captive (Acts 13:21-23). Luke 1:31-33 supports the fact that Jesus, the eternal king, will rule over Israel and over all nations. "And behold, thou shalt conceive in thy womb, and bring forth a son, and shalt call His name

JESUS. He shall be great, and shall be called the Son of the Highest: and the Lord God shall give unto Him the throne of His father David. And He shall reign over the house of Jacob forever; and of His kingdom there shall be no end."

The excellent news is that the Kingdom of Jesus Christ, who was in the line of David, will never end (Isaiah 9:6). This promise was an extension of the covenant given in Genesis 3:15. The promise consists of Jesus's resurrection and His exaltation to the right hand of God (Acts 2:29-33). In addition, there is the outpouring of the Holy Ghost (Acts 1:8) and His call to repentance (Acts 2:32-40), and Christ's kingship is described in the new heaven and the new earth (Revelation 21-22).

God is Sovereign and Supreme _____

The triune God — the Father, Son, and Holy Spirit — has all authority and dominion over things in heaven and earth. When God created man, He gave man authority over the earth and all that is in it. As our Heavenly Father, He has made provision through His Son, Jesus Christ, that all men can be born again and thus translated from the kingdom of darkness into the Kingdom of His eternal light. God has given every human being the right and authority to enter into His eternal Kingdom. Therefore, He calls you kings and has given you delegated authority to subdue and have dominion over the fish of the sea, the fowl of the air, the cattle, all the earth, and everything that creeps on the earth (Genesis 1:26). As kings you have authority, right, and influence in and over all the kingdoms and systems that are in the heaven and on the earth. Genesis 1:28 reads "and God said to them, be fruitful, and multiply, and replenish the earth, and subdue it: and have dominion over the birds that fly in the air, the animals and all that creep on the face of the earth." God is the supreme ruler and King of all kings. 1 Timothy 6:15 declares: "Which in His times He shall shew, who is the blessed and only Potentate, the King of kings, and the Lord of lords." He has the heart (spirit), soul, and body of the kings, queens, and governmental leaders in His hand. Proverbs 21:1 says: "The king's heart is in the hand of the LORD, as the rivers of water: He turneth it whithersoever He will."

Note, not in God's hands (plural) but God has all the kingdoms in His hand (singular). Yes, His single hand. God has humankind, religion, education, environment, entertainment, media, technology, government, and economy in His almighty hand. He set up times, seasons, and eons. He determines boundaries and horizons of people, places, and things. Daniel 2:21 reads: "And He changeth the times and the seasons: He removeth kings, and setteth up kings: He gives wisdom unto the wise, and knowledge to them that know understanding." It is God who will bring about all things in His own time. Our role is to seek the Kingdom of God for intimacy, direction, clarity, execution of purpose, and assessment of all God has placed in our hands to do.

What is God's spiritual Kingdom?
Kingdom is a realm, country, state, or territory

associated with or regarded as being under the control of a particular person or thing. Christ came to proclaim and bring to completion the spiritual Kingdom of God. There are several aspects of the Kingdom: Because Israel rejected Jesus, the **Kingdom in Israel** was taken away from them (Matthew 21:43). This passage is called parable of the husbandmen. Jesus the King, exemplifies the Kingdom and its power in the **Kingdom in Christ. The Kingdom in the church,** being born of the *water* and of the *Spirit,* prepares a man to see the **Kingdom of God** (John 3:3-5). The Kingdom signifies God's power reigning in the hearts and lives of all who repent and believe the gospel. The evidence of a believer's relationship with Jesus the King is that we receive His *righteousness, peace, and joy in the Holy Ghost* (Romans 14:17, 20). In essence, it isn't what a man eats or does not eat that brings righteousness, but what is in his heart.

The church has received great dynamos to assert itself against the dominion of Satan, sin, and evil. The Kingdom is manifested as a *powerful and forceful presence and action of God* in the midst of His people. In Mark 1:27 and following, the gospel reports that Jesus commanded with authority the unclean spirits, and they obeyed Him.

*What are the roles of a king in the earthly realm?*___

The king or queen has responsibilities to rule and have dominion over realm, country, state, or territory on the earth. What is *dominion*? In Hebrew the word is radah (raw-daw), which means to tread down or subjugate.

It also means prevail against, reign, rule over, or take over. In essence, kings or queens have domain and dominance over the people, places, and things in their spheres.

What is the role of kings in the Heavenly realm?

The Heavenly realm is called Kingdom of Heaven or Kingdom of God. When we speak of the Kingdom of God, we are referring to its authority in two time periods: this present age and a future age. The role of kings presently is to bring and manifest the Kingdom of God on the earth. What is the earth? The earth consists of the land and the sea kingdoms. We have dominion *on*, *below* and *above* the natural earth. The earth is made up of our land. For example, plains, valleys, hills, mountains, and plateaus. We also have dominion over the seas and everything in the seas. Further, we have authority in the atmospheric realm.

This is the prayer of Apostle Paul and the will, plan, and purpose of God that every believer receives the full revelation of God's redemption purposes in times past, present, and future. Our calling is a divine calling to assist Christ in bringing His Kingdom to earth. Ephesians 1:18-23 asserts: "That the eyes of your understanding being enlightened; that ye may know what is the hope of His calling, and what is the riches of the glory of His inheritance in the saints. And what is the exceeding greatness of His power to us-ward who believe, according to the working of His mighty power. Which He wrought in Christ, when He raised Him from the dead, and set Him at His own right hand in the heavenly places. Far above all principality, and power, and might, and dominion, and every name that is named, not only in this world, but also in that which is to come. And hath put all things under His feet, and gave Him to be the head over all things to the church. Which is His body, the fullness of Him that filleth all in all."

If you are not born again, please consider asking Jesus to be your Savior today. His ultimate desire is for you to enter into relationship with Him so that He can give you Himself. It is then that you can understand and exercise your kingly and priestly authority in heaven and on earth.

As powerful as King David was, he was not a perfect man. He could have provided better parental control over his family. He committed adultery with Uriah's wife and conspired to have Uriah killed in battle. Despite these shortcomings, David loved the LORD and repented of his sins and the LORD forgave him.

Chapter 5 — Questions to extend learning

What strategies can you implement to ensure that your marriage is adultery proof?

_____

_____

_____

_____

_____

Did your parents or someone else important to you reject and or abandon you? If so, how did you overcome the sting of abandonment?

_____

_____

_____

_____

_____

CHAPTER 6

A good life on earth and an inheritance for
Israel and the Christians

PALESTINE COVENANT — PALESTINE/ISRAEL'S LIFE CLASSROOM

- **The 6th Covenant — The Land Covenant (Deuteronomy 30:3) — unconditional covenant**

- **The 5th Dispensation — Law — (Deuteronomy Chapters 29-30)**

- **God made a promise to bless all of Abraham's seed. This includes Ishmael's seed and Isaac's seed.**

The Palestine Covenant is found in Deuteronomy 30:3. It speaks about the restoration and conversion of Israel. The book of Deuteronomy lays out the conditions under which Israel entered the land of promise. Note, during the Abrahamic covenant, the Israelites were never taken to the land (Genesis 12:2). Further, they haven't possessed the whole land (Genesis 15:18).

Numbers 34:1-12 describe the north, south, east, and west borders of the land of Canaan, which the children of Israel are to inherit. God instructed Moses in the plains of Moab by the Jordon to tell the children of Israel to drive out all the inhabitants of the land, destroy all their stone figures and molten images, tear down their high places (places of worship), and dispossess the inhabitants of the land. Then they were to dwell therein and divide the lots according to family size.

All choices have consequences _____

Deuteronomy 28 gives promises to God's people along with very stern warnings about the terrible things that will happen if the people do not keep their commitment. God wants to rejoice over His people to do them good and to multiply them but He wants the people to keep the words of the covenant from their side as well. Then He can establish His people and be their God. God instructed Moses: "But if ye will not drive out the inhabitants of the land from before you: then it shall come to pass, that those which you let remain of them shall be pricks in your eyes, and thorns in your sides, and shall vex you in the land wherein ye dwell" (Numbers 33:55). In other words, if the Israelites did not rid the land of its people who did not worship God, those people would create hardship for the Israelites. The LORD would allow their enemies to plague them and their seed because they did not carry out their commitment to Him.

Scattering the people of God _____

The Children of Israel learned that they were inadequate to keep the commandments of God. Also, they were afraid to trust God to provide, guide, protect, and lead them to the land of promise. In addition, they intentionally disobeyed God by worshipping idols and images in other religions. Deuteronomy 28:64 says: "And the LORD shall scatter thee among all people, from the one end of the earth even unto the other; and there thou shalt serve other gods, which neither thou nor thy fathers have known, even wood and stone."

The LORD disciplined the children of Israel by scattering them several times throughout history and putting them under the control of other nations: the Assyrians 722-721 B.C (2 Kings 17:6); the Babylonians 586 B.C, (2 Kings 25:21); the Greeks to Alexandria in Egypt in the 3rd century B.C.; and the Romans A.D. 70 (Luke 21:20-24).

Gentiles were in the plan of God from the beginning of time _____

Amos 9:9-15 speaks of blessings for Gentiles and Jews. In Acts 15:14-17, Peter addresses the council at Jerusalem to give clarity to the Jews that all mankind can be saved without being circumcised. Further Peter declared that God predetermined in the beginning of time that the Gentiles would come to hear the gospel, believe, and be saved by faith. And that's not all; the Gentiles also would receive the Holy Spirit just as the Jews did. He went on to explain that it is through the grace of the Lord Jesus Christ that Gentiles shall be saved, even as the Jews are the people of God. Afterwards, James answered, "Simeon hath declared how God at first did visit the Gentiles, to take out of them "a people" for His name" (Acts 15:14). More specifically, in Acts 15:16 we read: "After this I will return, and will build again the tabernacle of David which is fallen down; and I will build again the ruins thereof, and I will set it up that the residue of men might seek after the Lord, and all the Gentiles, upon whom my name is called, saith the Lord, who does all these things." Verse 18 continues: "Known unto God are all His works from the beginning of the world."

This is excellent news—we, the Gentiles, are not an afterthought. We were in the mind of God from the beginning of the world. The thoughts God thinks toward us are thoughts of good to give us all a favorable end (Jeremiah 29:11).

Restoration to the land _____

The LORD promised to gather up the scattered people and restore Israel to the land (Isaiah 11:11-12 and Jeremiah 23:3-8). More specifically, the LORD made a covenant that He would bring the children of Israel into the land that their father possessed. Ezekiel 37:21-22 says: "And say unto them, Thus saith the Lord God; Behold, I will take the children of Israel from among the heathen, whether they be gone and will gather them on every side, and bring them into their own land: And I will make them one nation in the land upon the mountains of Israel; and one king shall be no more two nations, neither shall they be divided into two kingdoms any more at all."

Hebrews 11:8-9 summarizes Abraham's faith journey and then verse 10 says: "For he looked for a city which hath foundations, whose builder and maker is God." Deep down inside, Abraham knew that the earthly

117

land of promise represented the eternal city of God. Revelation 21:1-7 speaks of the new and redeemed world where Christ lives with His people, the New Heaven and New Earth. Let's elevate our minds and set our affection on the heavenly righteous earth where all things are new. God will enjoy all those who receive Him in faith. This is the dwelling place where God invites all mankind, Jew and Gentile, to abide with Him.

National conversion

God vowed to circumcise the hearts of His people and their descendants (Hosea 2:14-16 and Romans 11:26-27). Gentiles and Jews are both considered the descendants of Abraham because of faith in Jesus Christ. Note, it is our Lord who took the responsibility to die for our sins and restore mankind back into right relationship through the new covenant.

National prosperity

"The LORD God will make thee plenteous in the work of your hand" (Deuteronomy 30:9).

Imperfect man but perfect, loving, and merciful dad

God's unending love, grace, and mercy brought each of His representatives back to Him. There were seven covenants God entered with an individual and/or nation. The people did not always obey God, yet God was able to cause everything to work out for His good.

He also demonstrated to the children of Israel that all the laws and ordinances could not be kept by man. God said He would institute a new covenant that would be based solely on the birth, life, sufferings, resurrection, ascension, return, and reign of Christ.

Here is a resource that you might finding interesting:

- The National Association for Ethnic Studies: ethnicstudies.org or call 804-828-2706

Chapter 6 — Questions to extend learning

God's chosen people rebelled against Him. How did God respond?

_____

_____

_____

_____

_____

_____

Please write the scripture that supports the fact that the Jews and Gentiles will inherit the new heaven and the new earth.

_____

_____

_____

_____

_____

_____

PART II

COVENANTS WITH THE NATIONS OF THE WORLD

❧❧❧

CHAPTER 7

Fathers mending broken relationships

THE NEW COVENANT — JESUS'S LIFE CLASSROOM

- **8th Covenant — The New Covenant (Hebrews 8:8) — unconditional covenant**

- **6th Dispensation — The Dispensation of Grace and the Church Age (John 7:37-39; cp. 1 Corinthians 12:12-13) Church (Acts 2:1) and (Revelation 19:21)**

The New Covenant is in Hebrews 8:8 and the 6th dispensation is found in Acts 2:1, John. 7:37-39, and also 1 Corinthians 12:12-13.

God's relationship with man is based upon covenantal relationships. To this end, you have read about renowned patriarchs and the children of Israel and their lives, struggles, and triumphs as they answered the call of God to save their lives and the lives of their families. An author writes for various purposes—to entertain, inform, or to persuade. To paraphrase Jeremiah 31:31-34, God made a new covenant with the house of Israel and Judah that He would put His law in their inward parts and in their hearts; which is man's spirit.

I have written this book to inform and persuade you to believe and receive Jesus as the Christ, the Son of the Living God. If you receive and accept this, you will live the God-kind of life on earth and spend eternity with Jesus.

*The law was given by Moses, but grace and truth were given by Jesus Christ*_____

Jesus is the bridge from the Old Testament to the New Testament. More importantly, Jesus is the bridge from the law to grace. Let me take you on this journey so that you can gain an understanding and be reminded about how much your Heavenly Father loves you.

Let's look at some of the benefits of knowing and entering a personal relationship with Jesus, your Christ! It is now possible to have true forgiveness of sins. Jesus is the mediator of this better covenant between God and man (Hebrews 9:15). Jesus's sacrificial death served as the oath or pledge that God made to seal us in this new covenant. In the Old Testament, the Ten Commandments were written on the tablets of stone, and Jeremiah 31:33 says: "I will put my law in their inward parts, and write it in their hearts; and I will be their God, and they shall be my people."

The announcement and declaration of the New Covenant affirms the following in Hebrews 8:10 NASB: "For this is the Covenant that I will make with the house of Israel after those days, says the Lord: I will put my laws into their minds, and I will write them on their hearts, And I will be their God, and they shall be my people." The school masters of the law have been replaced by faith and the grace of God through Christ in the New Covenant. Let's give God praise for the glory of His grace. In the Old Testament, Moses was a testimony or an example of the law, simultaneously demonstrating the need for grace and truth in the New Testament. To paraphrase John 1:17, "the law was given by Moses, but grace and truth came by Jesus Christ."

The Ten Commandments, which were the laws given to Moses, were inadequate to take away the sins of the Jewish people. The apostles were the original messengers, witnesses, and authorized representatives of Jesus. The Mystery of Christ was revealed by His holy apostles and prophets by the spirit. The mystery refers to the dispensation of the grace of God and the fellowship of the mystery. I will continue to focus on the dispensation of grace. For example, Apostle Paul wrote to the Church at Ephesus in Ephesians 1:6: "to the praise of the glory of His grace, wherein He hath made us accepted in the beloved." Although the Jews and Gentiles were both born in sin, the covenantal promise was made through and to the commonwealth of Israel. Salvation was extended to the Jewish people and then to Gentiles.

The Church Age: "A knock-out in Round One" _____

In Genesis 3:15 we read: "The Lord God said to the serpent: I will put enmity between thee and the woman, and between thy seed and her seed; he shall bruise thy head, and thou shalt bruise his heel." This means that there will be spiritual conflict between the "seed" of the woman which is the Lord Jesus Christ and the "seed" of the serpent and his followers.

124

"... that the blessing of Abraham might come on the Gentiles through Jesus Christ; that we might receive the promise of the Spirit through faith" (Galatians 3:14, Jeremiah 31:3). _____

After the death and resurrection of Jesus, the covenantal promises included the Gentiles who were at first without hope of salvation. Further, Jesus broke down the middle wall of the partition between us. He has made the Jews and the Gentiles both one. To paraphrase, God who is rich in mercy demonstrated His eternal love to the world. To this end, this invitation was given to all the dwellers of all the continents of this world. In addition, He made us alive together with Him, and it was by His eternal grace that we have provision for salvation.

I am grateful and ecstatic that we are living in the time that the prophets foretold. They told us of the mystery when salvation would be extended to the Gentiles who were strangers. Ephesians 2:8-9 reads: "For by grace are ye saved through faith: You cannot receive salvation without the grace of God empowering you to believe and receive His salvation from His Son." In essence, salvation isn't based on your works, penitence, devotion, medals, or faithfulness to a humanitarian group. More importantly, salvation is solely a gift of God.

The Covenant of Christ _____

The Bible wasn't written by the "white" man; it was written by men who were under the influence of the

Holy Spirit. We will focus on a few of the prophecies spoken by God through His spokespersons. 2 Peter 1:20 tells us that we must be aware of the fact that no prophecy of the scripture comes from someone's own interpretation, but the scriptures come from God. Then Hebrews 1:1 affirms that God's method of delivering His Word was in diverse manners through the prophets. Then God spoke through His chosen disciples/apostles who were witnesses to the life and work of Christ. Let's begin with the prophetic portraits of the character, perspective, and work of Jesus before He came to this earth.

Prophetic portrait of the messiah's character before He came to this earth _____

From the Old Testament, Isaiah 7:14 reads: "Therefore the Lord himself shall give you a sign; Behold, a virgin shall conceive, and bear a son, and shall call his name Immanuel." God kept and fulfilled His word. Matthew 1:21-23 reads: "and she shall bring forth a son, and thou shall call His name JESUS: for He shall save His people from their sins. Now all this was done, that it might be fulfilled which was spoken of the Lord by the prophet, saying, "Behold a virgin shall be with child, and shall bring forth a son, and they shall call his name Emmanuel, which is interpreted, God with us." Emmanuel came down from heaven to be with mankind. Let's also take a look at the name Jesus. "Jesus" is "Isous" in Greek and is the equivalent of the Hebrew "Yesua" (Joshua). The name means "Yahweh saves" or Yahweh is salvation. Salvation is the mission of Jesus.

126

Portrait of the character and work of Jesus while on earth _____

I am the Bread of Life (John 6)

The purpose of the gospels is to expose people to the light of Jesus. As a result, the world would believe in Christ and be justified by grace. God in the person of Jesus provides for man's natural needs. He promised to provide for our food, shelter, clothing — all our needs. Similarly, Jesus gave us His word which is spiritual food to energize our life. John 6:63 tells us the flesh needs the spiritual food. The Bible declares that man shall not live by bread alone but by every word that proceeds out of the mouth of God. Matthew 4:4 states: "It is the spirit that quickeneth; the flesh profiteth nothing: the words that I speak unto you, they are spirit, and they are life." In essence, God's word empowers human beings spiritually, physically, and mentally to live life to the fullest. As Jesus said, "my food is to do the will of my father who sent me and to finish His work" (John 4:34).

Christ brought life, liberty, and happiness, ensuring humanity's salvation.

You must put your faith in the sacrifice, crucifixion, resurrection, ascension, return, and reign of Christ in order to receive redemption. There are kingdoms and systems that comprise our world. The systems are humankind, religion, education, environment, entertainment, media, technology, government, and economy to name some. God created all systems and all systems are in subjection to God. All things exist through and by His intervention: Things that are seen and unseen, thrones, governments, dominions, principalities, and powers. Jesus's goal was to come into the systems in order to reveal God and His characteristics. Further, Jesus's goal was to identify with humanity's weakness and come alongside of us to present us to the Father as His dearly beloved children.

How did Jesus implement His authority in the earth?

In Matthew 4:12-16, Jesus's goal was to open up the blind eyes, therefore, He traveled to the coast of Capernaum, Naphtali, and the surroundings of Zebulon. This is the old border country of Zebulon and Naphtali. Jesus was prophecy fulfilled from Isaiah 9:6. This demonstration of the Kingdom of God was also spoken by Elijah. Matthew 4:16 describes the condition of the state of the people in Capernaum as representative of the position of humanity.

The residents' spiritual state was that they were blind and could not see clearly. In essence, they lived, walked, and breathed in darkness. They were rebellious against Jesus and marrying and divorcing without a cause. The government was an empire of evil, the tax collectors were dishonest, the religious system was overcharging the sincere and poor people during time of sacrifice, and the people were helpless. Everything about them exuded death and destruction. Sickness and disease were on the rise until Jesus showed up on the scene.

Jesus began to preach the words of freedom and light

and as a result, the bound people received the glorious light of Jesus. This was during the inauguration of Jesus's ministry. From this powerful revival, Jesus began to preach and to tell men to repent for the Kingdom of Heaven is at hand.

Christians, in order for your life and the life of your family, community, state, and the world to be changed, we must preach and live by the true gospel and means of grace! We must exemplify this light in our lifestyle because Christ is the true illuminator in a dark society.

I am a witness! Because Jesus Christ transformed my life ... _____

The Father has drawn me and empowered me to respond to accept Jesus as Lord and Savior of my life. He gave me a new life; it's called the new birth. I received Jesus's genes and DNA. I am proud of my heritage, yet now I have been transformed and translated as a child of light. I am daily assimilating to His eternal Kingdom. As I yield my mindset, temperament, characteristics, and personality to the power of the Holy Spirit, I become more like Jesus.

With this in mind, I am writing to persuade you to respond to Jesus so that you can be born again and receive a new life for yourself and your family. According to the Pew Research Center of the 6.9 billion people worldwide, 31.5% (2.18 billion) identify themselves as Christians. This is almost a third of the global population. Receiving Jesus gives you the ability to overcome the dominion of sin. Being a Christian doesn't make you perfect or sinless, but you are no longer under the dominion of sin and its power to control you. Recovering alcoholics have to persevere one day at a time and not live in fear that they will take the one forbidden drink and spiral back into the bondage of alcoholism. As Christians, we take it day-by-day as well, but the excellent news is that Jesus, our advocate, intercedes for us when we are standing strong in Christ as well as when we sin (1 John 2:1-2).

"Only believe"

To accept Jesus Christ, all you have to do is believe. Christians hold to Creeds which are confessions and symbols or statements of faith of shared beliefs. These beliefs guide the actions of the believers. The Latin word for Creed is *credo* which comes from *credere* which means "to believe." The Apostle's Creed and the Nicene Creed, two of the Christian Creeds, both start with "I believe" (in God). Christians saying these Creeds announce their belief and trust in God the Father, in the son Jesus Christ, and the Holy Spirit. Christians come to God through God's grace and through the redemption given by Christ who is our advocate. John 20:31 reads: "But these are written, that ye might believe that Jesus is the Christ, the Son of God; and that believing ye might have life through His name."

Be diligent in seeking your Creator and Father

You and I must come to God by faith. Hebrews 11:6 declares: "But without faith it is impossible to please

Him. For he that cometh to God must believe that He is, and that He is a rewarder of those who diligently seek Him." What does diligent mean? Diligence is characterized by steady attention. All people from any nation in the world who come to God must believe that God exists and that He gives benefits to those who consistently seek Him. Jesus is the express image of His person. Jesus is God incarnated in the flesh who came into this world. Thomas, a disciple of Jesus, went through the process of doubt in his Christian walk after Jesus's death. Thomas matured, and he overcame his doubt, attesting that "You are My Lord and My God" (John 20:28).

Living life forward by paying it forward _____

How is the spiritual presence of the Kingdom of God manifested in this present age? Matthew 6:10 holds this part of the Lord's Prayer: "Thy Kingdom come and thy will be done in earth as it is in heaven." The Christian's role is to follow our Heavenly Father's instruction by praying for the spiritual presence and manifestation of the Kingdom of God. The Kingdom is evident by asserting God's power in our family life, career, and ministry life. Our role is to go into the world systems through community service and jobs as well as create businesses and programs that are relevant for spiritual and social change for families locally and globally. The creative power of Jesus wants to flow through you and me to cast out devils and enable believers to speak with new tongues. Further, if we accidentally encounter a deadly serpent or unknowingly drink any deadly poison, Jesus's word declares that we will not be harmed. That's not all, Jesus commissioned His disciples to lay hands on the sick, and He promised that the sick will recover (Mark 16:17-18).

Jubilee: No more slavery in the earthly realm nor the spiritual realm

Jesus said, "I have come to proclaim the good news about freedom, I am the true liberator" (Luke 4:18-20). Christ wants you to know that He is your Jubilee; He will show you His favor. If you come to Jesus in faith, it doesn't matter what is in your bloodline, DNA, or what influences were passed down to you or your family members. His Spirit releases you from the proclivities and propensity of lying, stealing, cheating, hatred, jealousy, anger, debt, shame, guilt, pain, embarrassment, drug use, alcoholism, criminal activities, having children out of wedlock, recidivism, sexual perversions, gambling, pornography, and other addictions.

Jesus will forgive your past sins. He is the New Covenant. He has not and will not pronounce a curse on you or on your family. He will never sanction another human being to curse you. *You must believe that you are not cursed.* You have free will to do good and choose righteousness. He blessed you and your family from the beginning in the Garden of Eden during the Covenant of Edenic and the Dispensation of Innocence. That blessing is eternal. As a king and priest, He pronounced that you and your family be free by the power of the Holy Spirit, the word of God, the blood and the name of Jesus. He severed you from the spirit of helplessness,

powerlessness, and the spirit of victimization—
spiritually, emotionally, socially, mentality, vocationally,
physically, financially, and relationally.

Chapter 7 — Questions to extend learning

How did God take away humanity's sin and reconcile mankind back to Him?

_____

_____

_____

_____

_____

Please write the scripture that supports the statement that Jesus's goal was to open up the blinded eyes.

_____

_____

_____

_____

_____

A blissful life during the Kingdom Age

- **The Thousand Year Reign and the Kingdom Age**

- **7th Dispensation — the Millennium or Kingdom Age (Revelation 20:1-10)**

There are two great events that will prepare the Kingdom of God on earth. In the First Coming, called First event, Christ came as a savior (Matthew 1:21) and Second Coming, called the Second event, Christ will come as a judge (Revelation 20:10, 13-15, Matthew 3:12, and Luke 3:17). Christ has declared that the Kingdom of our God has become the Kingdom of our Christ.

The Kingdom in the consummation

This Kingdom refers to the Messianic Kingdom that was foretold by the prophets in Psalm 89:36-37. The Kingdom Age is the last of the ages of human life. Hence, Christ will rule and reign on earth as King of kings and Lord of lords for a thousand years (Revelation 20:4-6). This event is known as the 1,000 year reign. Also, the church will reign with Christ over the nations (1 Corinthians 6:2-3). At which point, the consummation of this promise will be fulfilled: The tabernacle of God is with men, He will dwell with them, they shall be His people, and God shall be with them and He shall be their God (Revelation 21:3).

According to the Life in the Spirit Study Bible, the Messianic Kingdom will terminate after a thousand years, and God's eternal Kingdom will be established in the new heaven and new earth (Revelation. 21:1-4). The center of the new earth is the Holy City, the New Jerusalem. Those who are born again will live in this Kingdom. Those who reject Christ will be judged then their punishment will be eternal fire. Oppression and misuse of government and religious power will end. This will be a time when death, sorrow, crying, and pain will cease. All these life challenges will be done away with for God's people. This is the Kingdom that was covenanted to David (2 Samuel 7:8-17). It is God's plan that all the families of the earth accept Him as Lord to reign with Him in the earth.

Future age

Portraits of the character, perspective, and work of Christ in Heaven _____

We must pray for Christ's return and for the establishment of God's eternal Kingdom in the new heaven and the new earth. Revelation 21:1-2 reads: "And I saw a new heaven and a new earth: for the first heaven and the first earth were passed away; and there was no more sea. And I, John, saw the holy city, New Jerusalem, coming down from God out of heaven, prepared as a bride adorned for her husband."

Chapter 8 — Questions to extend learning

How are you preparing for Christ's return?

_____

_____

_____

_____

_____

Please list 5 ways that you will share this book and message with others.

_____

_____

_____

_____

_____

_____

—PART III—

COVENANTS WITH MOREALE P. BROWN

∽∾

CHAPTER 9

Strategies to get out of toxic relationships

MOREALE'S LIFE CLASSROOM

- I am "infinitely loved"; I am of a generation which is infinitely loved by God, my Father. I do not represent the Baby Boomers; I identify with what I coined the "Infinitely Loved" Generation!

- Jeremiah 31:3 God said to me, I have loved you with an everlasting love.

- Psalms 136:3 My God's love for me is eternal!

- Smile — His love for you and me is infinite. Therefore, we are infinitely loved.

I am half a century young. In my opinion, my life is a publication. I am a testimony. I have lost three brothers and two childhood friends. I have come to know that all the good, bad, and the ugly you experience in your life's classroom are your lessons to make you a better person and to bring out the best in you. I am not minimizing traumatic experiences in my life or your life; I am declaring that you have lived through the worst of it. Now is your time to receive healing in order to be a healer of the families of the earth.

Broken relationship with my natural father

At moments when I was typing this book, I got a

little teary eyed. My mother told me that my father used to come by to pick me up to go buy shoes for me. During his visit, he wanted to have sex with my mother. After she resisted, he stopped coming to visit. This was painful for me. I do not remember his face or his smile. I don't remember what he smelled like. I do recall him being brown skinned. I do not remember my dad being affectionate, hugging, or rocking me to sleep. I cannot remember him playing and laughing with me. As you can see, my memory of my father is bleak. I am sure that most of you can identify and relate to my point of reference. Consequently, this is why I am so passionate about addressing the world-wide problem of fatherlessness.

God's unending love changed me. Have you come to learn about the unending love of God?

I could not end this book without writing about how He demonstrated His love and forgiveness toward me. Many people have a story about their experiences; this is my personal experience about what Jesus has done for me.

Jesus removed the consciousness of sin _____

I wanted to let know you know that God is a perfect God who loves imperfect people. He called me and has begun a good work in my spirit, mind, and soul. Although, I have failed Him during my Christian walk, He has never failed me. His message to

141

all men, women, boys, and girls who have sinned during their Christian walk is that He promises to forgive those who trespass against Him. Christ is the Christians' advocate. He died so that our past, present, and future sins can be forgiven. Please forgive yourself. Let Him take away your shame and receive His forgiveness.

No more toxic relationships _____

Earlier in this book, we looked at the relational circle. That included relationships with people, but not all relationships are healthy or helpful.

Have you ever tried to get out of a relationship that was detrimental to you, but the individual would make sure that they got involved with your family, friends, church, or work so that they could get back into your life?

I have decided to call my relationship perpetrator "G." When I would run out of the relationship and change my church, G would pop up at my new church. Also, when my mother and I moved, G found out the address and visited my apartment. G would act as if he was coming out of concern for my welfare.

Does it seem like when you are going to the next level spiritually that temptation comes?
G propositioned me and I accepted. My actions got me into a whole lot of trouble that I had to fight to get out of. So if anger, fighting, holding hands, kissing, or caressing gets you sexually aroused, then I strongly

urge you to "let it go." If you are hooked on pornography seek the mercy and grace of God to set you free. Hot or not, do not answer the call for a "booty call." Remember, free getaways aren't free. Do not look for the devil, he will look for you; but be vigilant and submit to God to resist the devil.

Here are a few strategies to implement to separate yourself from a bad relationship:

- Love yourself; identify and submit your weak spots to the Holy Spirit

- Change your numbers, residence if possible

- Mark their emails as spam

- Unfriend them on Facebook

- Possibly join another church, organization, or enroll in another school—if you need to do this, just do it!

- Get new friends

- Find a different/new restaurant or entertainment spot

- Most importantly, tell your family members and friends that under no circumstances are they to give out your contact information

Do you need a breakthrough to run out of a toxic relationship? _____

I needed a breakthrough to get the strength and courage to run from the toxic relationship. I used to see myself as a victim. "They did, they said, and they want" were in my thoughts. Now, I determine what I want and what I need in my life. I do not let myself think like a victim anymore.

When I meet someone, I ask my Heavenly Father if this person is supposed to be in my life and if so, what their purpose for being in my life is. My goal is to not mix and mingle with toxic people, but to keep them at bay. If a toxic person enters my life, I do not allow them in my private space. I will be cordial in public places, but I do not give them an invitation to become part of my inner circle.

Do you feel like you will never become free? _____

There were times when I got out of the relationship, but then I would fall right back into the pit. Then one day, G said, "Bad things are happening to you because we are in this relationship." It was at that point that I realized that I must get out and stay out otherwise the devil would use G to make me go to hell. Misery loves company so Satan doesn't care who he uses to kill you, steal from you, or bring destruction to you. At that point, it was like a competition rose up in me that I wasn't going to fall in Satan's pitfalls. I was determined to escape for good. If my memory serves me correctly, I slowly began to cut G off. Needless to say, G would throw a tantrum. He would say things like he was afraid I would leave him. He would be upset that I went somewhere with someone else, and he didn't know where I was. He also said that since I got my degree that I did not show my appreciation to him anymore. In spite of all this drama, it was only with the help of the Lord that I got out of that crazy situation. I began to yield myself to God and He delivered me!

How can you have healthy thoughts toward male/ females? _____

Although, I got out of the relationship and was delivered, it was difficult after that for me to have healthy relationships. I was delivered but becoming whole in my thinking took years. I had to develop new patterns of thinking and change my conduct. I remember Rev. Jackie McCullough saying in a sermon, "If you know that going left will get you into trouble, do not go left." To this end, I began to implement the strategy of "going right." I made the decision not to kiss in my relationships. I do not know what your challenges are, and I do not need to know; however, it is important that you know what leads you to trouble and that you make a conscious decision not to put yourself in harm's way.

What should you focus on in order to remain pure? _____

I began to ask myself where my tendencies and patterns come from. With respect to my family, I found out a lot about my background, which showed me where the tendencies developed. However, I learned not to blame my background but to take responsibility for my own thoughts, feelings, and actions. Once I had this under my belt, I was always engaging in personal

145

development and focusing on not sinning against God.

Then one day I heard Dr. A. R Bernard say, "If you are constantly saying, 'I am" not going to sin, I am not going to sin, I am not going to sin, I am not going to sin', then what is on your mind?" Sin! You are actually focusing on sin. When you focus on not sinning, it increases your chances of entering into sin. As the saying goes, you tend to go to the path of your most dominant thought. This information was empowering for me. It liberated me, and I do not focus on "fixing me" any more. I now focus on Jesus who is responsible for keeping me in order to present me to the Heavenly Father in the end time. I say to you, "Focus on Jesus and His word, stay under the protection of the blood, depend on the Holy Spirit, and call on the name of Jesus."

Religious curriculum _____

I have learned that God causes all things to work together for the good of those who love Him. I am glad to say, that He first loved me and has given me an opportunity to respond to His unending love. God has given parents the responsibility of teaching their children the Bible at home and partnering with a local church to reinforce Biblical teachings.

Our voices are what are needed in the world, so I urge you to use your talent, abilities, and gifts to help enrich others. I wrote this book to give you a clear picture of the unending love of our Heavenly Father. Please accept His eternal love today. Accept Christ as your personal Savior. Salvation is easy as A, B, C: A is for accept, B is for believe, and C is for confess. Now ask God to empower your decision.

Welcome to the family of God and the experience of the unending love of your Heavenly Father!

Chapter 9 — Questions to extend learning

Please describe a few strategies that you will use to separate yourself from your bad relationships.

_____

_____

_____

_____

_____

_____

What are the important principles to accepting Jesus as your Savior?

_____

_____

_____

_____

_____

_____

————————WORKS CITED————————

"Children on the Brink July 2004" *www.unicef.org/publications/index* (accessed September 20, 2014)

"Empowerment Skills for Family Workers" (Ithaca, New York G-09 MVR Hall, Cornell University Family Development Press 2003)

Goldsmith, M., Dr. "Leadership is a Contact Sport" *www.linkin.com.pulse* (accessed June 24, 2014)

John, T., Dr. Who's Pushing Your Buttons, Handling the Difficult People in Your Life (Nashville, TN) Thomas Nelson 2004

Lexical Aid to the New Testament

Merriam-Webster Dictionary *www.merriam-webster.com* (accessed September 20, 2014)

National Institute on Alcohol Abuse and Alcoholism, *www.niaaa.nih/gov/alcohol-health* (accessed March 1, 2015)

Thesaurus Wikipedia, the free encyclopedia *en.m.wikipedia.org/wiki/thesaurus* (accessed October 5, 2014)

"What are the seven dispensations?" *www.freerepublic.com/focus/f-religion* (accessed February 2, 2015)

en.m.wikipedia.org/wiki/interdependence accessed (March 2, 2015)

Unless otherwise indicated, scripture references in this book are from the Scofield Bible or the Life in the Spirit Bible. Paraphrased scripture to make a teaching point is so noted.

WORKS CITED

GLOSSARY

Apostles — the primary disciples of Jesus

Christian — a person who believes in Jesus Christ and follows His teachings

Church — a particular Christian group

Civic — relating to citizen, a city, or citizenship

Conscience — an aptitude, faculty, intuition, or judgment that assists in distinguishing right from wrong

Covenant — a sovereign pronouncement of God by which He establishes a relationship of responsibility

Conversion — change character, form, or function

Descendant — a person descended from another person, a relative directly related to a person

Dispensation — a period of time during which man is tested in respect to his obedience to some specific revelation of the will of God

Distinctiveness — the quality or state of being different

Dream — a series of thoughts, images, and sensations occurring in a person's mind during sleep

Economical — giving good value or service in relation to the amount of money, time, or effort spent

Everlasting — lasting forever, eternal, future life

Family — a group of relatives: a group of people who are closely related by birth, marriage, or adoption

Family background — information about a person's family — social, culture, education, work, religion

Fatherlessness — the absence of their father in children's lives

Fellowship — condition or relation of being in a friendly relationship; the fellowship of humankind

Free will — the apparent ability to make choices free from certain kinds of constraints

Friend — a person attached to another person by feelings of affection or personal regard; a person who gives assistance; a patron

Gentile — commonly means a non-Jew

Hardwired — determined by innate brain functions; not a matter of choice

Innocence — guiltless, a lack of guilt with respect to any kind of crime or wrongdoing

Interdependence — the mutual reliance between two or more groups; relationships where participants may be emotionally, economical, and/or morally reliant on and responsible to each other

Interpersonal — of or relating to relationships or communication between people

Jew — people who trace their origins through the ancient Hebrew people of Israel to Abraham.

Job — principal activity in your life that you do to earn money; occupation, line of work

Legacy — a gift of property, especially personal property, or money by a will; a bequest, anything handed down

Love — having a profound tender and/or passionate affection for another person

Moral — concerned with the principles of right and wrong behavior and the good or bad of human character

Nativity — process or circumstances of being born

Patriarchs — originally a man who exercised autocratic authority over an extended family; a man who heads a family, group, or government

Principles — general or basic truth on which other truths or theories can be based

Prophet — someone who brings a message from God to people

Realm — kingdom, sphere, land

Redemption — act of redeeming or atoning for a fault or mistake, or the state of being redeemed

Relationship — the way in which two or more people or organizations regard and behave toward each other

Religion — a belief or practice forming part of someone's thought about or worship of a divine being

Restoration — act of restoring, renewal, revival, or reestablishment

Skill Set — proficiency, facility, or dexterity that is acquired or developed through training or experience

Spirit — English word from Latin *spiritus* meaning "breath"

Stronghold — fortified place or fortress; a place of survival or refuge

Suitable help-meet — a person who is a helper or a person who is a good fit

System — an organized, purposeful structure that consists of interrelated and interdependent elements and entities

Unending — countless, continual, endless, never- ending

Wellbeing — good or satisfactory condition of existence, a state characterized by health, happiness, prosperity, and welfare

❦

————About the Author————

Reverend Moreale P. Brown is the President/CEO of Moreale Brown, Inc. As a high-impact educator, speaker, and author, she is in demand on an array of platforms.

Reverend Brown is a Certified Life Coach CPC, a member of the International Coaching Federation, a Certified Pastoral Member of the Sarasota School of Christian Counseling, and a Certified Member of the National Network of Toolbox Trainers through the Idaho Association Education of Young Children.

Reverend Brown believes that this book is a catalyst for fathers to return to God and turn to their families in order to bring healing and wholeness to their family (Malachi 4:6).

ॐ

For Bookings

Please contact Rev. Moreale P. Brown at 704-621-4860
or by email to infomoreale@gmail.com

We invite you to visit our website at
http://morealebrowninc.com